In *And Signs Shall Follow*, Gary Kinnaman presents a clear and comprehensive defense of charismatic teaching and practice. He avoids using personal testimonies which are often dismissed by non-charismatics as untrustworthy and subjective. Instead, Gary Kinnaman defends charismatic beliefs and practice from a systematic, doctrinal point of view. The result is this guide for both the charismatic seeking a well-reasoned response when questioned about his beliefs and the non-charismatic who desires to understand the scriptural evidence for the charismatic experience.

And Signs Shall Follow

Gary Kinnaman

Published by
chosen books

FLEMING H. REVELL COMPANY
OLD TAPPAN, NEW JERSEY

Scripture quotations are from the King James Version of the Bible. Italics throughout have been added by the author.

Baptism in the Holy Spirit: Command or Option? by Bob Campbell, copyright © 1973. Used by permission of the publisher, Whitaker House, Pittsburgh & Colfax Streets, Springdale, Pennsylvania 15144.

A Handbook on Holy Spirit Baptism by Don Basham, copyright © 1969. Used by permission of the publisher, Whitaker House, Pittsburgh & Colfax Streets, Springdale, Pennsylvania 15144.

"Inner Healing" by Steve Scott and Brooks Alexander, reprinted by permission of Spiritual Counterfeits Project, Inc., copyright © 1980. P.O. Box 4308, Berkeley, California 94704.

Gerhard Kittel and Gerhard Friedrich, eds., *Theological Dictionary of the New Testament,* Vol. 1 copyright © 1964 by Wm. B. Eerdmans Publishing Co.; Vol. 6 copyright © 1968 by Wm. B. Eerdmans Publishing Co. Used by permission.

Michael Hamilton, ed., *The Charismatic Movement,* copyright © 1975 by Wm. B. Eerdmans Publishing Co. Used by permission.

We are grateful to the Kenneth Hagin Ministries for use of their material, *Bodily Healing and the Atonement* by T. J. McCrossan.

Material reprinted from "Of Tidy Doctrines and Truncated Experience" by Robert Johnson, *Christianity Today,* February 18, 1977, is copyrighted by *Christianity Today* © 1977 and used by permission.

Material reprinted from "Evangelicals and the Inerrancy Question" by Kenneth Kantzer, *Christianity Today,* April 21, 1978, is copyrighted by *Christianity Today* © 1978 and used by permission.

Library of Congress Cataloging in Publication Data

Kinnaman, Gary D.
  And signs shall follow.

  "A Chosen book."
  Bibliography: p.
  1. Pentecostalism.   I. Title.
BR1644.K56   1987   234'.13   86-31413
ISBN 0-8007-9100-2

All rights reserved. No part of this publication may be reproduced, stored in a retrieval system, or transmitted in any form or by any means without the prior permission of the publisher.

A Chosen Book
Copyright © 1987 by Gary D. Kinnaman

Chosen Books are published by
Fleming H. Revell Company
Old Tappan, New Jersey
Printed in the United States of America

To my son
David

Special thanks to Pastor Charles McHatton, who guided me through my early years in charismatic ministry; to our church staff, particularly Kathleen Peterson, who assisted me with this project; to Rebecca Merrill Groothius, for her very helpful editorial suggestions; and especially to my wife, Marilyn, for being so patient with me during the extended writing and production of this book.

Contents

8 / CONTENTS

PREFACE

I am often approached by individuals who are hungry for more of the Holy Spirit, but who are entangled by theological objections to the baptism of the Holy Spirit, *per se,* and speaking in tongues. I have been at a loss to recommend a single book that faces the crucial issues with simplicity, clarity, and depth. A handy doctrinal reference is greatly needed.

For one man to presume to have all the answers is not wisdom, but ignorance. To answer adequately all the questions that have arisen over charismatic teaching and practice would be an impossible task. This book is simply an attempt to reply to the most common and significant objections to the movement.

And Signs Shall Follow is not a how-to presentation of charismatic truth. Of the writing of many books on tongues, healing, and spiritual gifts there is no end. But the vast majority of these books assumes that the reader is already open to receiving the baptism of the Holy Spirit. There is a crying need for a defense and clarification of charismatic theology for those who do not understand it. And we charismatics should know not only what we believe, but why we believe it.

Opponents of the charismatic renewal have published a number of well-researched books written by recognized scholars. With few exceptions, our response has been a mountain of testimonial literature, which only feeds the fires of our antagonists. We are constantly and condescendingly reminded, "You are arguing from your personal experiences, not from the Bible." In short, there is a demand for a sensible charismatic apologetic.

I realize that to a certain degree I am doing an injustice to the person and work of the One about whom I am writing. The Holy Spirit is able to defend Himself without the help of this publication. In fact, this is really what the charismatic renewal is all about! At the same time I feel compelled by the same Spirit "to give an answer to every man." My hope is that this book will add to the growing conviction that charismatic teaching is both biblical and reasonable, and that the supernatural manifestations of the Spirit are, indeed, for the Church today.

And Signs Shall Follow

Chapter One

Are Miracles
for Today?

THE CHARISMATIC RENEWAL has been the subject of one of the greatest theological and ecclesiastical controversies since the Reformation. This "latter-day outpouring" has created a spiritual explosion. Thousands have discovered a deeper spiritual life through the Pentecostal experience known as the baptism of the Holy Spirit, but not everyone agrees that this "move of the Spirit" is from God. As a result, serious and scathing criticisms have been leveled at charismatic believers, and much of the opposition has come from the ranks of Bible-believing, evangelical Christians.

What is the Charismatic Renewal?

"Charismatic" is derived from the New Testament Greek term *charisma*, translated "gift." Charismatic theology holds to a belief in a spiritual experience subsequent to salvation commonly known as the baptism of the Holy Spirit. This experience is usually accompanied by speaking in other tongues, or glossolalia, a term derived from the New Testament Greek word that is translated "tongue." The charismatic renewal is characterized by three things: the operation of the spiritual gifts described in 1 Corinthians 12 and Romans 12; the manifestation of the miraculous or supernatural; and dynamic, spontaneous praise and worship.

Bob Campbell writes that the baptism of the Holy Spirit is a doctrine that "has its roots in the Scriptures. It is not a new doctrine. The baptism of the Holy Spirit and the manifestation of the various gifts of the Holy Spirit were normal in the apostolic church. In fact, the New Testament was written by and for believers who were personally acquainted with every imaginable manifestation of the Holy Spirit's power, including the baptism, speaking in tongues, healing of the sick and casting out demons."[1]

It is deeply significant that this revival has not been limited to isolated and ostracized pockets of believers, but has swept every major denomination.

Kenneth Kantzer, a senior editor of *Christianity Today*, has described the breadth of the charismatic renewal:

> The most spectacular growth of evangelicalism, however, is to be found in the Pentecostal denominations and in the newer charismatic fellowships.....The modern Pentecostal movement came into being during the early part of this century. Until 1960, its influence was confined to small, splintered, and often despised sects on the fringe of mainstream Christianity. But in the middle and final thirds of our century, the charismatic movement really caught fire. In the last decade, it began to penetrate the mainline denominations, and now it is difficult to find a large congregation in any of the traditional church bodies of America unaffected by the char-

ismatic movement—even including many Roman Catholic churches.[2]

Christianity Today recently quoted David Barrett, editor of *World Christian Encyclopedia,* as estimating the number of Pentecostals and charismatics worldwide in 1985 at 150 million.[3] Millions of people have sought the baptism in the Holy Spirit and the demonstration of God's supernatural power—experiences common to first-century Christians. Yet many who oppose the charismatic experience think that the visible manifestations of the Spirit, particularly tongues, died with those early Christians. Let's see what the Bible says.

Biblical Evidence for the Charismatic Experience

The weight of biblical evidence favors those who believe that speaking in tongues, spiritual gifts, and the manifestation of the supernatural are to be an ongoing, integral part of the life of the Church. Nowhere does the Bible state directly that these special demonstrations of the Spirit will pass away sometime before Christ's return. The gospel of Christ has never been just one more great religious idea. It is a "demonstration of the Spirit and of power: That your faith should not stand in the wisdom of men, but in the power of God" (1 Corinthians 2:4–5). Anything less is not the *full* gospel.

The most commonly quoted Scripture on behalf of the Pentecostal experience is Acts 2:17: "In the last days, saith God, I will pour out my Spirit upon all flesh." The meaning of the phrase *last days* is key. This expression frequently refers to the final years of earth's history when the judgments of God will be poured out in unprecedented intensity (2 Timothy 3:1; James 5:3; 2 Peter 3:3). But the words "last days" are also used to describe the entire New Testament age, from the Pentecost to the Second Coming of Christ.

The writer of Hebrews, one of the first-century Christians, gives us a clear indication of the beginning of the "last days": "God, who at sundry times and in divers manners spake in time past unto the fathers by the prophets, Hath in *these last days* spoken unto us by his Son, whom he hath appointed heir of all things" (Hebrews 1:1–2). We know, then, that the "last days" actually began with the first coming of Christ.

The story of the first Pentecost reaffirms this early starting point for the "last days." Peter, under the direct influence of the Spirit, announced to those amazed by the events of that day that the outpouring of the Holy Ghost signaled the beginning of a new era, the "church age." He quotes the Old Testament prophet Joel:

> But Peter, standing up with the eleven, lifted up his voice, and said unto them, Ye men of Judea, and all ye that dwell at Jerusalem, be this known unto you, and hearken to my words: For these are not drunken, as ye suppose, seeing it is but the third hour of the day. But this is that which was spoken by the prophet Joel; And it shall come to pass in the last days, saith God, I will pour out of my Spirit upon all flesh: and your sons and your daughters shall prophesy, and your young men shall see visions, and your old men shall dream dreams: And on my servants and on my handmaidens I will pour out in those days of my Spirit; and they shall prophesy: And I will show wonders in heaven above, and signs in the earth beneath; blood, and fire, and vapor of smoke: The sun shall be turned into darkness, and the moon into blood, before that great and notable day of the Lord come: And it shall come to pass, that whosoever shall call on the name of the Lord shall be saved.
>
> Acts 2:14–21

The "last days," then, which will culminate with the Second Advent, began on Pentecost.

Some claim that Peter's use of Joel's prophecy was merely an "illustration" of what was happening on the day of Pentecost.[4] But Peter, inspired by the Spirit, preached emphatically, *"This is that* which was spoken of by the prophet Joel" (Acts 2:16). Peter could have qualified his statement and said, "This is *like* that which was spoken of by the prophet Joel." But he did not! Peter firmly believed that the events of Joel's prophecy were specifically and literally fulfilled on the day of Pentecost and were signs of the "last days."

In the days that followed, Peter did not change his theology. After the miraculous healing of the crippled man at the gate of the Temple, he continued to be convinced that the Old Testament prophets were speaking of the Church age. "Yea, and *all the prophets* from Samuel and those that follow after [including Joel], as many as have spoken, have likewise foretold of *these days"* (Acts 3:24).

Thus, if the "last days" may be defined as the days from Pentecost to the Second Coming (Acts 2:17; Hebrews 1:1-2), and if the Spirit is to be poured out "in the last days" (Acts 2:17), then the outpouring of the Holy Spirit evidenced by tongues and other spiritual gifts is for the Church from Pentecost to the Second Coming. For this reason Paul wrote in his "charismatic" epistle, 1 Corinthians, "Even as the testimony of Christ was confirmed in you: So that ye come behind in no gift [Greek: *charismati*]; waiting for the coming of our Lord Jesus Christ . . . " (1 Corinthians 1:6-7). The gifts of the Spirit will not fail until Christ returns.

"In the last days, saith God, I will pour out my Spirit on all flesh." The present-day outpouring could not be more timely. Intellectualism, materialism, neo-orthodoxy, humanism, and modernism have cut the heart out of the Bible, and the consequence has been the entrance of other gods—the gods of spiritism, transcendental meditation, astrology, and the occult. In the aftermath of an age of skepticism God is restoring to the Church the demonstrative power of the Holy Spirit to counter those who oppose the authority of the Bible.

In the days of the first apostles, when the revelation of the New Covenant was resisted and those who believed it were persecuted, God shut the mouths of His opponents by a show of the Spirit's supernatural power. Similarly, in this present time when confidence in the absolute authority of the Bible has been abandoned, God is stopping the mouths of the critics by visible signs of the Spirit's power. DeVern Fromke writes: "In this hour when men skilled in their natural gifts and abilities are fainting, God is awakening many to see how imperative it is to expect the supernatural."[5]

Most recently, a growing "Signs and Wonders" movement has emerged, the so-called "third wave" of evangelical renewal following this century's first wave of Pentecostal renewal early on, and a second charismatic wave beginning around mid-century. Dr. C. Peter Wagner, professor at Fuller Theological Seminary in Pasadena, has noted in *People of Destiny* magazine "the moving of God among mainline evangelicals who are neither Pentecostal nor charismatic, yet operate with the same kind of power."[6]

An intellectual defense of the Bible is always helpful, but in itself it is insufficient. We must grasp the truths of the Scriptures with our hearts as well as our minds. Additionally, the truth of the Scriptures must be affirmed by the demonstration of the Holy Spirit (see Mark 16:20). The apostle Paul understood the necessity of the supernatural confirmation of God's Word when he wrote of his critics: "I will come to you shortly, if the Lord will, and will know, not the speech [*logos*, that is, the teaching or doctrine] of them . . . but the power" (1 Corinthians 4:19).

Certainly Christian doctrine is vital, but apart from the anointing and power of God's Spirit the great doctrines of Christianity are meaningless. Paul says that "the preaching of the cross is to them that perish, foolishness" (1 Corinthians 1:18). The anointing of the Spirit brings both enlightenment *and* confirmation. The Holy Spirit not only opens my mind so that I can understand the Word (1 Corinthians 2:13–14; John 16:13); He also demonstrates that the Word is true by working miracles to prove it!

The Church today is rediscovering this long-dormant Holy Spirit power, and an unprecedented, phenomenal expansion of the Church internationally is being attributed to this new surge of the supernatural. In a recent article entitled "Where in the World Is the Church Growing?" Sharon Mumper reported for *Christianity Today:* "Healings, exorcisms, and other supernatural signs and wonders have accompanied phenomenal growth of the church not only in China, but in many other surprising parts of the world. In fact, the church around the world is growing in ways that have seldom before been seen."[7]

Arguments Against the Charismatic Experience

Even in the light of scriptural evidence supporting and confirming the fact that signs and wonders will be given in these last days, those who take issue with the charismatic experience raise two questions. The first is, "Do we need really charismatic gifts, since we have the Bible?" and second is, "Don't we see in Scripture itself that miracles were beginning to decline toward the end of the first century?"

This first argument, whether or not we need the visible

evidence of the Spirit, is based on 1 Corinthians 13. Paul writes that "when that which is perfect is come, then that which is in part shall be done away" (verse 10), at which time tongues will cease (verse 8). Many sincere Bible teachers believe that the coming of the perfect thing in this passage is a prophetic reference to the completion of the writing of the New Testament Scriptures. In other words, once God's men finished writing the Bible, the perfect thing came and the charismatic gifts ceased because they were no longer necessary.

But those who teach that "the perfect" is the Bible are obscuring the clear meaning of the passage. Let's read further:

> For we know in part, and we prophesy in part. . . . For now we see through a glass, darkly; but then face to face: now I know in part; but then shall I know even as also I am known.
> 1 Corinthians 13:9, 12

To what, then, does "the perfect" refer? This expression—literally, "the perfect thing" or "perfection"—points to the Second Coming of Christ, when at last we shall no longer peer through "a dark glass," but we will see Him "face to face" (verse 12). Revelation 22:4 confirms that only in eternity will the saints "see his face." At that time, prophecy, tongues, and our limited knowledge will cease.

Even though we have the Bible, God's written revelation, we must concede that *now* (in this present age) we know in part, and we see "through a glass, darkly." We do not have full knowledge or understanding, and no student of Scripture, regardless of how long he has studied the Bible, can claim to have seen Christ "face to face." When our Lord promised to send the Comforter who would teach us all things (John 14:16, 26), He was not referring to a book. The Bible undeniably is our only standard of life and doctrine, but the canonization of the New Testament is not even remotely implied in 1 Corinthians 13.

Opponents of the charismatic renewal carry this point further to claim that not only the gifts, but miracles, too, are unnecessary today because we have the Bible, God's final word to man. Yet many of the same fundamental and evangelical churches that protest contemporary miracles on these grounds have recently been beset by theological controversy over the inerrancy of the Bible.[8] It seems that they have failed to recognize that doctrinal debate alone will never prove the divine inspiration of the Bible. By minimizing the manifested power of God's Spirit, many of these church bodies have rejected the very weapon that will win the war against the skeptics of biblical inerrancy.

The second question about seeing the decline of miracles in Scripture itself is based on one particular verse: 2 Timothy 4:20. In this verse we are told that Paul left his brother Trophimus "ill at Miletus." Since one person was not instantly healed by the power of God, that is allegedly proof that the age of miracles was waning.

But we must remember that the message of healing, miracles, or tongues is never an absolute guarantee that everyone who hears will respond and receive. Not everyone in the Bible continually experienced a life of miracles. Trophimus, knowing the healing power of God, was left sick. Multitudes in the New Testament, hearing the Word of God, were left without salvation. Even Jesus was not able to perform miracles when the spirit of unbelief prevailed (Mark 6:5–6). But the failure and unbelief of men can never make void the promises of God (see Hebrews 4:2 and Romans 3:3–4). God will always have a believing remnant, and He will always be a miracle-working God. "Jesus Christ the same yesterday, and today, and for ever" (Hebrews 13:8).

If Jesus is always the same, then the power of Christ through which an apostle healed a man crippled from birth (Acts 3:1–6) is the same power of Christ through which we witness astounding miracles in ministries like that of the late Kathryn Kuhlman. Perhaps those who cannot embrace the charismatic renewal themselves can confess with Gamaliel, "Refrain from these men, and let them alone: for if this counsel or this work be of men, it will come to nought: But if it be of God, ye cannot overthrow it; lest haply ye be found even to fight against God" (Acts 5:38–39). With similar openness to the evidence of Jesus' miracle-working power, an ignorant man, once blind from birth, put to shame the Jewish theologians: "Whether he [Christ] be a sinner or no, I know not: one thing I know, that, whereas I was blind, now I see" (John 9:25).

Later even those leaders of the Jews confessed after Pentecost, "What shall we do to these men? for that indeed a notable miracle hath been done by them is manifest to all them that dwell in Jerusalem; and we cannot deny it" (Acts 4:16).

Miracles are especially for today. If there has ever been a time in the history of the Church when miracles were needed to confirm God's Word, it is now. Miracles will never save souls, but they do confirm the reality and authority of God's Word.

Chapter Two

Old Testament Roots of Pentecost

A FULL UNDERSTANDING of Pentecost is not possible without a careful study of its Old Testament roots. We err if we try to understand Pentecost only in retrospect, for just as the Old Testament points to our need for the Messiah, we find it also broadens our understanding of the need for a separate encounter with the Holy Spirit. Let's look at two major revelations: first, how the Old Testament festivals relate to Pentecost; and second, the Old Testament concept of the anointing.

The Old Testament Festival Calendar

The outpouring of the Holy Spirit was a stunning new phenomenon, but Pentecost as a Jewish holiday was not. The fact that the outpouring of the Spirit occurred on that particular feast day was not coincidental. There were three major Old

Testament festivals: *Passover, Pentecost,* and *Tabernacles* (see Leviticus 23). I would like to suggest that these Jewish festivals disclose the triune being of God and His relationship to mankind in each of His Persons.

Passover, a springtime celebration commemorating freedom from the bondage and slavery of Egypt, speaks to us of the sacrificial death of Christ. When Jesus broke bread with His disciples at the Last Supper, which was the Passover meal, He was replacing the Old Testament festival with a "New Testament Passover." While recalling the sacrifice of lambs, through which God had spared the Israelites, He pointed to the shedding of His blood once and for all, for the sins of the entire world. Jesus was the ultimate Passover Lamb.

Passover also included two other festivals: Unleavened Bread and Firstfruits. During Passover week, Israel was to cleanse its households of leaven, which speaks of sanctification. Firstfruits seems to be prophetic of the resurrection of Christ. This ceremony took place "on the morrow after the sabbath" (Leviticus 23:11), the "eighth" day. Furthermore, Paul declares that Jesus has "become the firstfruits of them that slept" (1 Corinthians 15:20). He is the first to be resurrected, and, as such, is the assurance that we shall be also. Passover also initiates the Jewish festival year; it is the starting point. This, too, would seem to point to Jesus, who is the initiator of our faith.

One could debate the meaning of much of the symbolism of the Passover week, yet it is unmistakably a celebration of and experience in the second Person in the Trinity, Jesus Christ.

Pentecost was scheduled to be observed fifty days after the Passover, and was established to celebrate the entrance into the Promised Land after Israel's forty years in the wilderness. The Holy Spirit, the third Person of the Godhead, is associated with Pentecost, not by analogy so much as by history.

There are, however, some subtle connections. Perhaps the seven weeks between Passover and Pentecost, or seven times seven, speak of the completeness of the comprehensive work of salvation in the Son and in the Spirit, suggestive of Paul's words to Titus: "According to his mercy he saved us, by the washing of regeneration [Passover, the work of the Son], and renewing of the Holy Ghost; Which he shed on us abundantly [Pentecost, the work of the Spirit] through Jesus Christ our Saviour" (Titus 3:5–6).

Leviticus 23:17 is especially instructive of the spiritual meaning of Pentecost:

> Ye shall bring out of your habitations two wave loaves of two tenth deals: they shall be of fine flour; they shall be baked with leaven; they are the firstfruits unto the Lord.

The "two wave loaves" are central in the celebration of Pentecost. "Two" is a biblical number, which speaks of witness and testimony. Jesus sent out his disciples two-by-two, the book of Revelation speaks of the two great witnesses (11:3–4), and we are counseled that in the mouth of two or three witnesses every word should be confirmed (2 Corinthians 13:1). What did Jesus tell His disciples about Pentecost? "Ye shall receive power, after that the Holy Ghost is come upon you: and ye shall be witnesses unto me" (Acts 1:8).

The two loaves may also symbolize the witness of Jews and Gentiles being bound together by the Spirit of God. The Holy Spirit will be poured out on "*all*" flesh," according to the prophecy of Joel. Moses describes this as "fine flour," ground together and "baked with leaven." "Leaven" certainly would be an appropriate allusion to the Gentiles being bought into the family of God. Christ was the firstfruit, the single sheaf waved before the Lord during Passover. These two loaves are the firstfruits of the harvest of the Spirit.

When unraveling Old Testament symbols like this, we can never be absolutely certain about their meaning, especially when they are not specifically interpreted in the New Testament. However, of this one thing we have no doubt: Pentecost is the festival of the Holy Spirit. This was the day chosen by the Godhead for the Spirit to be poured out in power. As Passover is an experience in the Son, so also Pentecost is a unique and distinctive experience in the Spirit.

The final festival, Tabernacles, takes place in the autumn of the year and represents the end of the Jewish religious calendar. This festival of finality also incorporated Trumpets and the Day of Atonement. Tabernacles was particularly eschatalogical, for in its celebration of the harvest and its positioning at the end of the religious year, it pointed forward to the end of the age.

Zechariah refers to Tabernacles in association with the Day of the Lord and the Messianic Kingdom: "Behold, the day of the Lord cometh. . . . Then shall the Lord go forth, and fight against those nations. . . . And his feet shall stand in that day upon the mount of Olives. . . . And it shall come to pass, that every one that is left of all the nations which came against Jerusalem, shall even go up from year to year to worship the King, the Lord of hosts, *and to keep the Feast of Tabernacles*" (Zechariah 14:1, 3–4, 16).

The concurrent festivals of Trumpets and Day of Atonement also seem to point to the consummation. Throughout the New Testament the trumpet sound signals the *parousia*, the Second Coming (see Joel 2:1). Furthermore, the Day of Atonement represents a national reconciliation with Yahweh, a kind of judgment day, if you will. Passover, in contrast, was individual and familial.

Tabernacles points to the Second Coming of Christ, but it also points to the Father, the first Person of the Godhead. We naturally associate the throne of judgment with the Father, for the Lamb (Christ) stands beside the throne (Revelation 4–5; 22:3). Just beyond the Second Coming of Christ is the moment at the end of the age when God the Father becomes all in all. Paul writes of this mystery:

> All (shall) be made alive. But every man in his own order: Christ, the firstfruits [Passover: the glorified Lamb]; afterward they that are Christ's at his coming [Pentecost: those whom the Holy Spirit has made alive]. Then cometh the end, when he shall have delivered up the kingdom to God, *even the Father* [Tabernacles: the consummate revelation and experience of God]. . . . And when all things shall be subdued unto him, then shall the Son also himself be subject unto him that put all things under him, *that God may be all in all.*
> 1 Corinthians 15:22–24, 28

It should be fairly clear at this point, debate over details aside, that the Jewish festival calendar provides a framework for understanding: one, the nature of the triune Godhead, and two, that a distinctive experience of each of the Persons of the Godhead awaits the believer. God is one, yet the Bible makes a clear distinction among the Persons of the Trinity. Similarly, we may also make a differentiation within our personal experience of each Person of the Godhead.

God has revealed Himself as Father, Son, and Spirit; this is how He is known. I suggest that He cannot be fully known without a corresponding revelational encounter with each of the Persons of His divine being. Passover points to a revelational, personal encounter with the Son; Pentecost points to a revelational, personal encounter with the Spirit; and Tabernacles points to a revelational, personal encounter with the Father. There is overlap because God is essentially one, but there must also be differentiation because God has revealed Himself as triune.

Pentecost is the encounter with the abiding Comforter who strengthens and sustains the Church from the time of the Passover, the sacrifice of Jesus for us, to the time of Tabernacles, the consummate experience of God Himself, when "God will be all in all." It is within this framework that a separate and distinctive experience in the Spirit is not only biblical, but necessary for each believer. Pentecost as an experience in the Spirit must be both harmonized and differentiated from Passover, the experience of the Son.

Pentecost and "the Anointing"

As we look further into Old Testament roots, we find a second basis for a separate and special encounter with the Spirit. This is the biblical, particularly Old Testament, concept of the anointing. Throughout the Old Testament, the anointing was a symbol of the Holy Spirit *upon* that person's life for the purposes of leadership, ministry, and service. This Old Testament practice of pouring out oil upon selected persons points forward to the outpouring of the Holy Spirit on Pentecost.

The New Testament introduces the new concept of the Spirit *within*, which produces the fruit (Galatians 5:22–23). Jesus Himself predicted that the Spirit would be *in* us (John 14:17), an idea readily accepted by the Christian community today. We believe that at the time of initial salvation when we ask Jesus into our hearts, the Holy Spirit comes to dwell *within* us.

But the New Testament also vigorously upholds the Old Testament idea of the Spirit *upon* us, and this shows our need for a subsequent encounter with the Spirit. Jesus said, "You shall receive power, after the Holy Spirit has come upon you, with the result that you shall be My witnesses." This suggests that the Spirit upon us is for leadership and ministry, while the Spirit within reproduces the character and virtues of Christ. Thus, we see the need for the anointing power of the Holy Spirit to come upon us as well as dwell within us if we are to serve Jesus fully.

The Person and ministry of Jesus illustrate these two aspects of the Holy Spirit. He who was conceived by the Spirit (born of the Spirit, we could say), and thereby infused through His being by the life of the Spirit (the Spirit within), grew in stature and in favor with God and man (see Luke 2:52).

Before Jesus entered ministry, He was a man of true biblical holiness, but this in and of itself was not sufficient to qualify Him for leadership and ministry. It was not until the Holy Spirit came upon Him that the government was placed "on His shoulder" and He began His ministry of teaching, preaching, healing, and performing many other miracles. Jesus immediately affirmed His calling to public ministry on the basis of the Spirit upon Him, not on the basis of His wonderful, godly life (the Spirit within).

> The Spirit of the Lord is upon me, because he hath anointed me to preach the gospel to the poor; he hath sent me to heal the broken-hearted, to preach deliverance to the captives, and recovering of sight to the blind, to set at liberty them that are bruised, To preach the acceptable year of the Lord.
>
> Luke 4:18–19

Similarly, when He commissioned His disciples after His resurrection, He commanded them to wait in Jerusalem, to do nothing in ministry, until the Spirit had endued them with power—the Spirit *upon* (Luke 24:49), the Old Testament idea of a special anointing.

Jesus had the Spirit *within* and *upon*. The early Church had the Spirit *within* and *upon*. Both aspects are essential— the former to reproduce the character of Christ (the fruits), the latter for authority and power in leadership and ministry (the gifts).

D. L. Moody had some interesting things to say about this distinction. In his book *Secret Power: Or the Secret Success in Christian Life and Work,* he wrote:

> The Holy Spirit dwelling in us, is one thing: I think this is clearly brought out in Scripture; and the Holy Spirit upon us for service is another thing. . . .
>
> I think it is clearly taught in the Scripture that every believer has the Holy Ghost dwelling in him. He may be quenching the Spirit of God, and he may not glorify God as he should, but if he is a believer on the Lord Jesus Christ, the Holy Ghost dwells in him. But . . . though Christian men and women have the Holy Spirit dwelling in them, yet He is not dwelling within them in power; in other words, God has a great many sons and daughters without power. . . .
>
> People see that we are carrying around empty buckets, and they will not come to us until they are filled. They see we haven't any more than they have. We must have the Spirit of God *resting upon us,* and then we will have something that gives the victory over the world, the flesh, and the devil; something that gives the victory over our tempers, over our conceits, and over every other evil. . . .
>
> Then, the Holy Spirit *in* us is one thing, and the Holy Spirit *on* us is another; and if these Christians had gone out and went right to preaching then and there, without the power, do you think that scene would have taken place on the day of Pentecost? (italics mine)[1]

This is not an isolated quotation; it expresses the theme of Moody's entire book. Admittedly, he does not mention the charismatic gifts specifically, but the implication of his statements to the doctrine of the baptism of the Holy Spirit as a second and special experience is most significant. This renowned man of God realized that there is more to the ministry of the Holy Spirit than is taught in many churches today.

Almost one hundred years ago, F. B. Meyer wrote:

> May we, ordinary Christian people, living in this nineteenth century, hope to receive the Holy Spirit in that extraordinary and especial measure in which He rested upon Elijah? Of course we have all received that Holy Spirit to a certain extent, or we could never have come to Jesus. All the graces of the Christian character, all our comfort, all our overcomings, are due to His presence. And yet it is clear that over and beyond this ordinary grace, which all believers must have, there is a blessed anointing of the Holy Ghost which gives special equipment and fitness for service.[2]

In summary, two Old Testament observances, the festival calendar and the common practice of anointing with oil, provide a framework for every believer to understand the outpouring of the Holy Spirit. The festivals explain the need for a special, identifiable experience with each Person of the Trinity, and Jesus Himself is an example of the Old Testament pattern of anointing. His life and ministry represent the two aspects of the work of the Spirit: the Spirit *within,* for the development of character and spiritual fruit; the work of the Spirit *upon,* for ministry and the release of the spiritual gifts.

The Old Testament is our starting point, but it is only a shadow. The fullness of the Spirit is fully revealed in the writings of the new covenant, so let's look carefully at the New Testament teaching on this wonderful experience known as the baptism of the Holy Spirit.

Chapter Three

The Purpose of the Baptism

JESUS COMMANDED His disciples "that they should not depart from Jerusalem, but wait for the promise of the Father.... And he said unto them ... ye shall receive *power*, after that the Holy Ghost is come upon you: and *ye shall be witnesses unto me*" (Acts 1:4, 7–8). The Greek word translated "power" is the term from which we derive our English word dynamite. Don Basham writes, "The baptism of the Holy Spirit is not a saving experience for the non-Christian; it is an empowering experience for the Christian, in order that he may be supernaturally equipped to perform his ministry."[1]

But someone may respond, "Is it not true that anyone who tries to win souls for Christ will manifest the power of the Holy Spirit mentioned in Acts 1:8?" Yes and no. The statement "Ye shall be my witnesses" has been misunderstood to mean simply that every Christian *should* go out and witness. Though it certainly implies this, there is a much deeper meaning. Notice carefully that Jesus did not say, "Ye shall go out and witness." He declared, "After that the Holy Ghost is come upon you . . . ye shall *be* witnesses unto me." There is a vast difference between the activity of witnessing as a religious obligation, and *being* a witness to the powerful, life-transforming ministry of the Spirit of God. The promise to the disciples that they would *be* witnesses was fulfilled on the day of Pentecost, not by passing out Gospel tracts, nor by Christian philosophizing, but by a mighty and miraculous outpouring of the Holy Ghost. So great and unusual was the manifestation of the Spirit on the day of Pentecost that three thousand were converted. The disciples became witnesses of Christ as the Spirit worked wonders through them.

The evangelistic method of exhibiting the power of the Holy Ghost was not confined to Pentecost. Paul affirmed the necessity of spiritual power when he reminded the Thessalonians, "Our gospel came not unto you in word only, but also *in power, and in the Holy Ghost*" (1 Thessalonians 1:5). To the Romans he wrote of his ministry that the gospel message was confirmed "through mighty signs and wonders, by the power of the Spirit of God" (Romans 15:19). And to the Corinthians he declared, "And I, brethren, when I came to you, came not with excellency of speech [polished oratory]. . . . My speech and my preaching was not with enticing words of man's wisdom, *but in demonstration of the Spirit and of power*" (1 Corinthians 2:1, 4). And these "sign" gifts are not to be limited to the ministry of the first-century apostles. According to 1 Corinthians 12, the special manifestations of the Spirit are for the entire Body. "The manifestation of the Spirit is given to every man" (1 Corinthians 12:7).

"These *signs* shall follow *them that believe*" (Mark 16:17).

Christianity is more than just another religious philosophy. Signs are to demonstrate to a world enamored of its own religious systems that Jesus Christ alone is the way, the truth, and the life (John 14:6). A manifestation of the Holy Ghost and power is not to be equated with polished oratory, successful debate, a well-organized message, or a convincing apologetic. Although the Spirit certainly uses such things, ultimately faith is not to rest in the abilities and wisdom of man, but in the power of God. We are limited in our witnessing if we don't realize this. Though sharing and preaching are absolutely necessary to the communication of the message of salvation (Romans 10:14), the gospel is not to be given "in word only," not with "enticing words of man's wisdom, but in demonstration of the Holy Ghost and power [*dunamis*]."

The baptism of the Holy Spirit is a source of divine power. Even the Lord Jesus would not lift a finger in ministry until the Spirit of God descended upon Him (Matthew 3:16; 4:12–17). Similarly, our Lord did not hastily send forth his disciples immediately after the resurrection. Instead, Jesus commanded them to tarry in Jerusalem and wait for the promise of the Spirit. D.L. Moody wrote emphatically:

> I venture to say that there are very many who, if you were to ask them, "Have you received the Holy Ghost since you believed?" would reply, "I don't know what you mean by that." They would be like the twelve men down at Ephesus, who had never understood the peculiar relation of the Spirit to the sons of God in this dispensation. I firmly believe that the church has just laid this knowledge aside, mislaid it somewhere, and so Christians are without power. . . . The great question before us is, "Do we want it?"[2]

The baptism of the Holy Spirit is also a gateway to a deeper spiritual dimension. This is evident in four key areas for Christians today.

First, the baptism of the Spirit releases the spiritual gifts in the life of the believer. It is interesting to note that the nine gifts listed in 1 Corinthians 12:7–12 are actually called "manifestations of the Spirit." We must be careful to distinguish between "gifts of the Spirit" and natural abilities. Howard Snyder writes:

> Each person is born with latent potentialities which should be developed and employed to the glory of God. This is stewardship. But when the New Testament speaks of spiritual gifts, it goes beyond this. Paul says the Holy Spirit "apportions to each one individually as he wills" (1 Corinthians 12:11). This suggests a direct and immediate relationship between God and man through conversion and life in the Spirit. The gifts of the Spirit result from the operation of the Spirit in the life of a believer, and so are something more than merely the wise and faithful use of native abilities. Gifts must be understood as, literally, *gifts* of the *Spirit*.[3]

When charismatics practice the presence of the Holy Spirit, they are permitting and promoting the operation of these supernatural gifts. There is no doubt the manifestations listed in 1 Corinthians 12—healing, miracles, prophecy, tongues—are supernatural in character, which leads to the question: Of the churches that resist or reject the present-day supernatural outpouring of the Holy Spirit, how many evidence these manifestations of the Spirit? Or, all evidence aside, how many even understand them? Yet believers who accept the baptism of the Holy Spirit as a special grace are consistently characterized by signs following.

Notice I am basing this observation on the Word of God.

The New Testament Church was a "charismatic" community in the sense that it "[came] behind in no gift [*charismati*]; waiting for the coming of our Lord Jesus Christ" (1 Corinthians 1:7). The early Church did not "despise prophesyings" (1 Thessalonians 5:20), nor did it forbid speaking in tongues (1 Corinthians 14:39). The gifts and the power behind the believers, namely the Holy Spirit, were not hindered and restricted by theological misunderstanding and doctrinal rigidity.

Second, the baptism of the Spirit unlocks a deeper relationship with Jesus. Through it the Lord Jesus Christ is revealed and exalted. Charismatics have frequently been accused of exalting the ministry of the Holy Spirit when they should be lifting up Christ. The truth of the matter is, however, that when the Holy Spirit is given a free hand, He will not speak of Himself, but will testify of Christ (John 15:26). This is precisely what is happening in the charismatic renewal.

Third, the baptism of the Spirit exposes the evil power of Satan. One of the charismatic gifts is the discerning of spirits (1 Corinthians 12:10). Many have testified that after receiving the baptism of the Holy Spirit their awareness of the reality of Satan and his devices intensified. Scriptures such as "For we wrestle not against flesh and blood, but against principalities, against powers, against the rulers of the darkness of this world, against spiritual wickedness in high places" (Ephesians 6:12) suddenly become clear after one experiences the baptism of the Holy Spirit. Mere theory becomes a practical and invaluable guideline in ministry. Even though a person may believe in the existence of the devil, in practice he may view the work of Satan in general terms, as an impersonal force. Unable to pinpoint the work of the enemy, unable to identify specific spiritual snares and spirits of oppression, many of God's people cannot resist the forces of evil effectively. Hence, the need for discerning of spirits, a charismatic gift.

Consider Jesus and His disciples in relation to satanic influence. We could hardly classify them as passive or indifferent. They were not ignorant of Satan's devices. Without fear or unbelief, and without superstition, they confronted Beelzebub and were victorious. Current attitudes in the Church toward the power of Satan do not always parallel those of the first-century Church. Charles Usher writes:

> Unbelief is clever at self-justification. How it reasons! "The Lord has withdrawn His miraculous gifts; they were intended only for the early church; the days of miracles are over. It is not the work of the Church of God today to cast out demons or heal the sick. We are in a different dispensation than when the Acts of the Apostles was written. The miraculous supernatural power of Pentecost has been withdrawn."
>
> Has Christ withdrawn His power, or is it dammed up by our unbelief?
>
> Are tortured souls to languish in the hell of suffering while we look on, helpless to aid their deliverance?
>
> Bound souls all around us are crying out for liberation from the grip of the enemy who is holding them in bondage. What answers are we giving them?[4]

It is only logical to assume that a greater awareness of the supernatural—signs, manifestations, miracles, wonders of the Holy Spirit—will be accompanied by a greater insight into the devices of Satan. For this reason I believe that the reality of the baptism of the Holy Spirit has become a spiritual battleground in the Church today. Through the mighty effusion of the Holy Spirit, eyes are being opened to the realm of the supernatural—good *and* evil. It is no wonder that the charismatic renewal is being vigorously opposed, and no wonder that within the ranks of the movement there is excess and abuse. If on the one hand Satan cannot prevent us from embarking on the ship of truth, he will do everything in his power to push us overboard.

We will address the gift of tongues specifically later, but I want to include something here that Arthur Wallis affirms:

> The devil knows that there is authority in the right use of this gift [speaking in tongues], but I believe he fears it, not so much because of what it is in itself, but because, manifested as it was on the day of Pentecost, it is a symbol of the power and gifts of the Spirit in this age, the weapons that God has given us to plunder the strong man's house. . . . Perhaps this is why Satan has attacked this gift so vehemently and relentlessly, seeking to corrupt and spoil it on one hand, and to despise and vilify it on the other.[5]

"For the weapons of our warfare are not carnal, but mighty through God to the pulling down of strongholds" (2 Corinthians 10:4).

Fourth, the baptism of the Holy Spirit sheds a new light on the Word of God. Paul writes that God has "made us able ministers of the new testament; not of the letter, but of the *spirit:* for the letter killeth, but the *spirit* giveth life" (2 Corinthians 3:6). The Bible is not an end in itself. Its purpose is to reveal the Person of Christ and God's eternal plan, that "he might gather together in one all things in Christ" (Ephesians 1:10). The Bible is not just a book of systematic doctrine, though we have tried to systematize it. Nor is it merely a book of philosophical theory, though philosophers have pondered its profundity. The Bible is primarily a book of practicalities. It is the Book of *Life,* and the "Spirit giveth life."

The Holy Spirit never lifts us into a realm of mystical experience where the Bible loses its significance and authority because the Spirit of the Lord is Word-oriented. The Bible has been inspired by the same Spirit who imparts the charismatic gifts. Consequently, the importance of the Word is not minimized by charismatic teaching, it is intensified.

Though the benefits are manifold, the baptism of the Holy Spirit is not a formula for instant spiritual success. The baptism does not automatically make one a better Christian, nor does it place the recipient on a higher spiritual level than one who has not received. But the baptism does release the power of the Spirit in the life of the believer. It creates the potential for the operation of the charismatic gifts and launches the Christian into a new dimension of spiritual warfare. Most important, the fullness of the Spirit results in a vibrant and powerful exaltation of the Lordship of Jesus Christ.

Chapter Four

Must the Baptism Be Sought?

MANY HAVE OBJECTED to the charismatic quest for the Spirit because, supposedly, the New Testament is silent about "seeking the baptism." I find, however, that there are two significant reasons for this spiritual pursuit: One, religious tradition has obscured the truth of the Pentecostal experience; and two, the Scriptures *do* teach that we are to seek the Spirit and His gifts. We will examine first the matter of religious tradition.

The outpouring of the Spirit, evidenced by speaking in tongues, should be the spontaneous sequel to repentance and conversion, a truth accepted without controversy by the early Church.

In Acts 2:38 Peter declares, "Repent, and be baptized . . . for the remission of sins [salvation], *and* ye shall receive the gift of the Holy Ghost [the baptism of the Spirit]." This conclusion to Peter's sermon on the day of Pentecost is paralleled

41

by Hebrews 6:1–2: "Let us go on unto perfection [or maturity]; not laying again the foundation of repentance . . . and of faith toward God [salvation], of the doctrine of *baptisms* [plural]." This doctrine of baptisms includes baptism in water *and* baptism into the Holy Spirit, both of which *follow* repentance and faith, just as Peter proclaimed in Acts 2:38.

In Acts 8 we again find this same pattern. Philip went down to Samaria "and preached Christ unto them. And the people with one accord *gave heed unto those things* which Philip spake . . . [and] they *believed* [salvation] Philip preaching the things concerning the kingdom of God, and . . . *were baptized.* . . . Now when the apostles which were at Jerusalem heard that Samaria *had received the word of God* [another reference to initial salvation], they sent unto them Peter and John: Who . . . prayed for them, *that they might receive the Holy Ghost:* (For as yet he was fallen upon none of them)" (verses 5–6, 12, 14–16). Again we see the scriptural pattern set for us here: (1) initial salvation, (2) baptism in water, (3) baptism into the Holy Spirit.

Paul's salvation experience was no different in that baptism in the Spirit occurred after his conversion on the Damascus road. Acts 9:1–9 tells of how Paul surrendered his life to the Lord Jesus Christ and three days later, when Ananias in obedience to the command of the Lord laid his hands upon him, Paul received the Holy Spirit (Acts 9:11–12, 17).

Some years later when Paul preached the gospel in Ephesus (Acts 19:1–2) he met some disciples who had *believed* (salvation), but had not yet received the Holy Ghost. In fact, they had not even heard of the Holy Ghost! The divine Comforter surely must have been working in their hearts for them to be receptive to the coming Messiah, although they had not yet received the gift, the promise, the full manifestation of the power of God's Holy Spirit. "And when Paul laid hands upon them, the Holy Ghost came on them; and they spake with tongues, and prophesied" (verse 6).

Titus 3:5–6 is another New Testament Scripture that is significant in this regard. In these verses we read that the Lord "saved us [total salvation experience], by the washing of regeneration [initial salvation], *and* renewing of the Holy Ghost [baptism of the Holy Spirit]; Which he shed on us abundantly. . . ." The Greek term rendered "shed on" is more correctly translated "poured out." In fact, elsewhere in the New Testament whenever this term is used to describe the Holy Spirit it *always* refers to the Pentecostal experience. The baptism or "renewing" of the Holy Spirit was part of the total salvation experience that God purposed for all His people. (See Acts 2:17–18, 33; 10:45. Interestingly, in the last instance, the Holy Spirit was poured out on the Gentiles immediately after they believed on the Word. It was a sign to the astonished Jews that they had indeed received salvation, and should, therefore, be allowed to be baptized in water in the name of Jesus.)

The new believers in the early Church and the ministers who led them into the salvation experience were not of the same frame of mind as are preachers and converts today. In our day the baptism of the Holy Spirit is misunderstood, ignored, and even rejected.

The outpouring of the Holy Spirit as an identifiable New Testament experience has been lost, and like anything else that has been lost, it must now be sought and found. This is not to imply that the baptism of the Spirit is not readily and graciously available to all who ask, but that it has become veiled by centuries of spiritual and theological blindness. The baptism of the Spirit is, unfortunately, no longer that spontaneous sequel to salvation. It has been veiled and spurned even as the vital doctrines of *sola fide* and *sola scriptura* were veiled and rejected for better than a thousand years. The light of the Holy Spirit has been hidden under an ecclesiastical bushel. Don Basham writes, "Years of wrong teaching and biblical ignorance . . . leave a psychological barrier that creates difficulty in receiving the baptism, even after we are intellectually convinced it is real."[1]

In some ways, attitudes in the Church today toward the charismatic renewal resemble the doctrinal rigidity of the scribes and Pharisees of the first century. The religious leaders of the Jews actually missed the first coming of Christ because of their inflexible interpretations of the Old Testament. Writes Bob Campbell: "All too often when God has wanted to do something, *religious* people have been the ones to oppose Him. In fact, *religious* people were responsible for the death of Jesus. The scribes and Pharisees studied the Word of God thoroughly, but instead of conforming their minds to it, they conformed the Word to their doctrines and traditions. They rejected God's Son (even though He healed the sick and raised the dead), because He told them things that conflicted with their doctrines and traditions. Men are the same today, putting more faith in denominational doctrine than in the words of Jesus."[2]

In the paragraphs that follow I have evaluated two contemporary statements, examples of the kind of teaching that quenches Pentecostal fires.

Robert Gromacki, a strong opponent of the charismatic movement, writes: "The Spirit did not come as an answer to apostolic prayers or the laying on of hands, but at the sovereign appointed time of the Father. Thus, the event was unique and *can never be repeated*" (italics mine).[3] What a declaration! It implies that believers are in error when they "seek the baptism" because the Spirit in the book of Acts moved sovereignly, apart from human desire or reason. Aside from ignoring the biblical reasons for seeking the Holy Spirit, which I shall discuss shortly, this statement further implies that not only do our requests for the baptism fall on deaf ears, but that the Spirit of God does not move sovereignly in any charismatic outpourings today. The remarkable rise and advance of the charismatic renewal is, in my opinion, evidence that He does.

Another critic writes, "One can imagine the psychological and spiritual tensions which a teaching of this sort [seeking the baptism] creates. . . . I have read of instances where people have become mentally ill because they failed to receive."[4] In response I offer the following observations.

First, such reasoning appeals to our emotions, not the Scriptures; in this sense it avoids the issue.

Second, as I have indicated, the "spiritual tensions" to which this writer refers are probably the result, at least in part, of those who resist the charismata, not those who promote them. The sword of the Gospel (Matthew 10:34–36) brings a division, a schism initiated not by those who believe, but by those who continue in unbelief.

Third, the baptism of the Holy Spirit is a promise, not a reward. In all fairness, tensions can also be blamed on those unloving and legalistic Christians who, though sincere, put too much pressure on others to receive the Spirit and speak in tongues. In some circles, speaking in tongues is actually considered a prerequisite for salvation; one cannot get to heaven without it. However, in spite of these errors, one is not summarily excused from responding to the truth just because that truth has been mishandled by an unwitting few.

And fourth, throughout the Scriptures we find exhortations to grow, mature, change, and develop in spiritual things. The command "Be ye holy; for I am holy" (1 Peter 1:16) certainly could lead to spiritual tensions. But this does not mean that we are to ignore the exhortation. Similary, 1 Corinthians 14:1 tells us that we are to desire earnestly the spiritual gifts. Should we ignore this injunction simply because there is the possibility that it may give some Christians psychological fits? God forbid! Religious tradition has obscured the truth of the charismatic experience, but it is real, nonetheless. This brings us to our second major reason for seeking the baptism: The Scriptures clearly teach us to.

In Luke 11:9–13 we read, "Ask [that is, keep on asking], and it shall be given you; seek [keep on seeking], and ye shall find; knock [keep on knocking], and it shall be opened unto you. For every one that asketh receiveth; and he that seeketh findeth; and to him that knocketh it shall be opened. . . . If ye then, being evil, know how to give good gifts unto your children; how much more shall your heavenly Father give the *Holy Spirit* to them that ask him?"

Notice first that this verse is speaking of a father's relationship to his children. This refers to God's relationship to believers, those who already possess a measure of the Holy Spirit. Second, the children are asking their father for a gift. The gift according to the context is specifically the Holy Spirit. Interestingly, the Pentecostal outpouring is also called "the *gift* of the Holy Ghost" (Acts 2:38). We see from this directive that we as believers—who already possess a measure of the Holy Spirit—are to keep on seeking the Holy Spirit, and our Father will hear and answer our prayers with a special gift. I do not accept the view that this promise, as well as select other portions of the Gospels, are dispensationally limited to national Israel and are not for the Church.[5]

In Acts 19:2 Paul asked the Ephesian disciples, "Have ye received the Holy Ghost since ye believed?" Was not the apostle implying by this statement that those who had not received the Holy Spirit should ask and seek? In response to Paul's question and in fulfillment of Luke 11:9–13, they asked and received; they sought and they found. The Father gave His children the *gift* of the Holy Spirit.

Paul commands us in 1 Corinthians 14:1 to "desire spiritual gifts." *The Amplified Bible* renders this text, *"Earnestly desire and cultivate the spiritual endowments."*[6] The context of the surrounding chapters deals with the charismatic gifts. Here we are told to seek them.

Some believe that the commands in 1 Corinthians 12:1, 31 and 14:1 to "covet earnestly" the gifts are not exhortations (imperative in the Greek: "You must covet the gifts"), but merely statements of fact (indicative: "You are coveting the gifts"). Certain present imperative and indicative forms in the Greek as in this case are identical. Paul, critics say, was not teaching the Corinthians to seek the gifts; he was sarcastically criticizing them for it. According to this view Paul was saying, "You are selfishly coveting the spiritual gifts, but I will show you a more excellent way—love." However, if this had been Paul's intention, then he probably would have used the emphatic pronoun *humeis*, "you yourselves" and the conjunction *alla*, "but," and not *kai*, "and," which appears in the Greek text. If these grammatical changes were made, then and only then would the resulting translation read: "You *yourselves* are seeking the spiritual gifts, *but* I show unto you a more excellent way." Yet this is not what Paul wrote. The verb *zeloute* ("earnestly desire") is a commandment, not a statement of fact. To my knowledge there is not a single English translation or standard Greek authority that understands *zeloute* to be a mere statement of fact. Why? Because the meaning of the Greek grammar here is obvious—*zeloute* is a commandment.

Yet those who accuse charismatics of ignoring or misusing Scripture have themselves mistranslated this verse to prove their point that Paul's words are not commanding us to seek the gifts of the Spirit. In a Bible conference I attended some years ago, a sincere, well-known man, president of a reputable evangelical seminary, used this very interpretation as a basis for his refutation of the charismatic renewal. Whether or not he still holds this view I do not know, but it also appears in print in a popular book criticizing the renewal.[7]

Even if critics are not satisfied that these Scripture references teach us to seek the Spirit and His gifts, they must concede that the Bible does not tell us to *avoid* the charismata, as some would like us to believe.

Howard Ervin comments:

> So often the blanket assumption is made that the Christian is not to seek the gifts of the Spirit. It is frequently phrased something like this: "If God wants me to have them, He will give them to me." On the surface, this affirmation sounds convincingly pious. Actually, it is merely platitudinous. There is a rather obvious error in the tacit assumption that grace operates irresistibly upon the passive, even indifferent child of God. The ancient Psalmist, for instance, knew nothing of such pious self-deception when he sang: "As the hart panteth after the water brooks, so panteth my soul after thee, O God, My soul thirsteth for God, for the living God."[8]

God won't force the baptism and accompanying gifts upon us, but He is a good Father and will give generously if we ask. The Scriptures are clear about that. And they are just as clear that He wants us to seek this wonderful gift as an experience subsequent to salvation.

How Long Before We Receive?

But there is yet a probing question we must answer: How long after salvation should one expect to wait before receiving the promise of the Spirit? At this point we come face-to-face with two extremes: classical Pentecostalism and rigid fundamentalism. On the one hand there is an overemphasis on what has been called the "second blessing" theology, while on the other hand there is a total rejection of any teaching that even suggests a special work of the Holy Spirit.

The Word of God presents a balance between these two extremes. As I have demonstrated, the gift or promise of the Holy Spirit is a distinguishable experience, a truth that has been obscured through nearly two thousand years of Church history. Since its rediscovery, the controversy over whether or not it is valid has caused us to lose sight of the timing between the events of initial salvation and the outpouring of the Holy Spirit.

The baptism of the Holy Spirit is a unique New Testament experience subsequent to salvation, and it should be *immediately* subsequent. Once the Spirit was poured out at Pentecost, the disciples did not encourage waiting a long interval of time between initial salvation and receiving the Holy Spirit. As a matter of fact, for the three thousand new converts on the first Pentecost, repentance, water baptism, and baptism into the Holy Spirit all took place on the same day.

The baptism of the Holy Spirit is a gateway, not a goal, and thus should occur as soon as possible after salvation. Even the Lord Jesus Himself, in order that all things might be fulfilled, received a special outpouring of the Holy Spirit immediately after being baptized in water (Luke 3:21–22). And He, of course, is the pattern Son.

The giving of the Holy Spirit, like everything else in the Christian life, is by grace through faith. The gift of the Spirit is a promise. Jesus said He would send the Spirit because of what He has done, not on the basis of our personal righteousness or spiritual achievement. The Holy Spirit has been given to the Church and is readily available to all who ask in faith.

Thomas Smail writes:

> The New Testament assumption is that all Christians are in the full experiential flow of the Spirit's life and power, because in being initiated into Christ they have come to know the full release of the Spirit as well. In Samaria and at Ephesus, there were believers for whom this was not so, but far from being typical, they were the *subnormal exceptions* with whom urgent measures had to be taken to bring them up to spiritual par, which means not some second experience beyond Christ, but the appropriation of all that has already been offered them in him (italics mine).[9]

The work of Christ and the work of the Holy Spirit are one. The Scriptures identify the baptism of the Spirit as a distinctive and subsequent experience, but at the same time they leave no room for a theology that excavates a canyon between initial salvation and the baptism. Nor should the idea of a "second blessing" be overemphasized.

The baptism of the Holy Spirit is a unique gift, ready to join initial salvation and baptism in water in one glorious, transforming moment for the believer. "Repent, *and* be baptized . . . for the remission of sins, *and* ye shall receive the gift of the Holy Ghost" (Acts 2:38).

Chapter Five

What Is Glossolalia?

SPEAKING IN TONGUES is supernatural communication with God through the Holy Spirit. Don Basham has defined this gift as "a form of prayer in which the Christian yields himself to the Holy Spirit and receives from the Spirit a supernatural language with which to praise God."[1] Paul wrote: "For he that speaketh in an unknown tongue speaketh not unto men, but unto God: for no man understandeth him; howbeit in the spirit he speaketh mysteries" (1 Corinthians 14:2).

Speaking in tongues involves both a natural and a supernatural element. On the day of Pentecost "the Spirit gave them utterance," yet *they* did the speaking (see Acts 2:4; 19:6). Many have doubted the genuineness of their own experiences in the Holy Spirit and have said, "When I spoke in tongues, it was just me." In one sense, that is true! The salvation experience serves as an illustration of this. When a person first meets Christ, the Holy Spirit must bring conviction into his heart. Yet at the same time, that individual himself must be willing to ask Christ to take control of his life. He must open the door of his life and allow Christ to enter. This may or may not result in an emotional experience. So it is with the baptism of the Holy Spirit. He fills us, but we must be willing to move our tongues.

Tongues Are Languages

Tongues are often identifiable languages. This special kind of miracle, whereby one is able to speak fluently a language he has never learned, first occurred on the day of Pentecost. In Acts 2:6–11 we read, "Now when this [speaking in tongues] was noised abroad, the multitude came together, and were confounded, because that every man heard them speak in his own language. . . . 'We do hear them speak in our tongues the wonderful works of God.' " There are hundreds of contemporary examples of this Pentecostal miracle that could be shared. Ralph Harris alone reports seventy-five documented contemporary cases of glossolalia in languages recognized by hearers but unknown to speakers.[2] Don Basham[3] and Dennis Bennett[4] have recorded many other examples.

But more often, tongues are unidentifiable as any known language. It is this aspect of glossolalia that has caused skeptics to subject it to the scrutiny of linguistic experts, and their observations have been quoted by those in opposition to the modern tongues movement. For example, Gromacki writes: "The conclusion of the linguists indicates that modern glossolalia is composed of unknown sounds with no distinguishing vocabulary and grammatical features, *simulated* foreign features, and the *total absence of language characteristics*" (italics mine).[5]

On the one hand, Pentecostals and charismatics believe that tongues are languages; on the other hand, critics retaliate that speaking in tongues is mere gibberish. How do we explain this contradiction?

Glossolalia Is Supernatural Communication

Some humorous but pointed remarks by Marcus Bach are in order:

> "If you can speak in tongues, let me hear what it's like."
> The challenger was Dr. Grant Fairbanks who had recently received his Ph.D. in speech pathology and was now on the university's psychological staff. An expert in the field of aural rehabilitation, he sat in on several of our off-campus group discussions but was never on hand "when the Spirit came through."
> I could not blame the Spirit for its reluctance to appear when Dr. Fairbanks was around. This young phonetician had an uncompromising dedication to the strictly scientific approach. He had no patience with unmeasurable speculation, and his studies, rigidly tied to theoretical calculation, social disturbances, mental distortions and the like, were enough to close the doors on any Pentecostal winds. I was sure, at this stage of the game, that when the Lord said, "Prove me now," He did not mean He would accept the challenge of a "show-me" specialist in speech. He meant instead that He wanted a show of faith. Dr. Fairbanks contended, however, that if there was anything to glossolalia, it should be possible to take it into the laboratory, subject it to a psychophysical study and wrap the whole thing up in a neatly scientific package under systematic test control.[6]

Though I strongly disagree with much of Bach's book, his comment on the futility of applying the scientific method to the things of the Spirit is to the point. First Corinthians 2:14 tells us that "The natural man receiveth not the things of the

Spirit of God: for they are foolishness unto him: neither can he know them, because they are *spiritually* [not intellectually, not naturally] discerned."

Tongues are "languages" of the Spirit, and as such are spiritually discerned. Speaking in tongues is a form of supernatural communication with God. I prefer to use the term *communication* instead of *language*, because language consists of words, letters, grammar, and linguistics—characteristics of human speech. But linguistic symbols are not the only means of communication. For example, husbands and wives can communicate by facial expressions. An infant communicates by crying. In our technological age human language is converted into the language of computers.

Linguistics is only one of many methods of communication. Paul writes of the inner, speechless groanings of creation, of our spirits, and of the Holy Spirit (Romans 8:22–26). We are also told that God knows the very thoughts and intents of the human heart. Communication with God is not limited to speech in the linguistic sense; tongues do not have to be language as we know language. Numerous references in the Bible support this view.

First Corinthians 14:14, for example, teaches that "if I pray in an unknown tongue, my *spirit* prayeth, but my understanding is unfruitful." Speaking in tongues is primarily spiritual communication, making use of, but not limited to, human language.

Another example is 1 Corinthians 13:2. In this verse Paul makes reference to the languages of men *and of angels*. Because angels are spiritual beings their method of communication, or language, is spiritual. There is no reason to assume that the languages of angels even remotely resemble, linguistically, the languages of men. A speech expert would have no point of reference if he were to submit the languages of angels to human analysis. Some may protest, "Is not language itself a creation of God? And should we not therefore expect the languages of men to be at least an imperfect representation of language as God first ordained it as a vehicle of human communication?" Yes, we have been created in the image of God and language is one of His gifts to us. Yet in one sense, the inadequacies of human language as we know it may also be considered a punishment! When the languages of men were confused at the Tower of Babel, there was a communication breakdown. Human languages corrupted by sin may be no better a representation of the languages of heaven than our corruptible bodies are representations of what we shall be in the resurrection.

Mark 16:17 is another relevant verse: "These signs shall follow them that believe... they shall speak with *new* tongues." The Greek term translated "new" is significant. There are two Greek words rendered "new" in our English Bibles. The first, *neos*, means new in time, while the second, *kainos*, means new in kind. It is this second word, *kainos*, that is used here in Mark 16. Arndt and Gingrich, foremost Greek authorities, write that the usage of *kainos* in Mark 16:17 is to be understood "in the sense of something not previously present, *unknown, strange, remarkable*, also with the connotation of marvelous or *unheard-of*" (second italics mine).[7] Here in Mark 16 it is predicted that those who believe in Christ would speak in *"unheard-of"* tongues.

In Acts 2:12-13 we discover two entirely different reactions to glossolalia. "And they were all amazed.... Others mocking said, These men are full of new wine." On the one hand, some were amazed to hear their own languages being spoken, while others mocked. We assume one hundred and twenty spoke in tongues, yet there are only fourteen languages identified in Acts 2. Those who mocked probably heard no known language, only what sounded like ecstatic utterance. In Kittel's incomparable Greek dictionary, Johannes Behm writes, "There would be no occasion for scorn if unknown (human) languages were spoken intelligibly."[8] This passage of Scripture demonstrates clearly that sometimes glossolalia is recognizable human language, sometimes it is not.

In addition to the above Scripture references, Greek authorities almost without exception list "ecstatic speech" as one of the definitions of *glossa*, which is the Greek term translated "tongues." In this regard, Gromacki concludes in his survey of Greek authorities "that linguistic scholars regard the phenomenon of glossolalia as being foreign languages and ecstatic utterances, with primary emphasis and application on the latter."[9] Included in Kittel's dictionary is the statement: "In Corinth, therefore, glossolalia is an unintelligible ecstatic utterance. One of its forms of expression is words or sounds without interconnection or meaning."[10] I contend that the sounds are "without interconnection or meaning" not because glossolalia is mere gibberish, but because speaking in tongues is supernatural communication with God. It is speech in the Spirit—sounds that are unintelligible and meaningless to the natural man.

Tongues Will Cease, But When?

Along with the linguists' stand against the authenticity of tongues, scholars have argued that tongues—identifiable or unidentifiable—have ceased, and base this on a study of the Greek verbs in 1 Corinthians 13:8. The verse reads: "Charity never faileth: but whether there be prophecies, they shall fail; whether there be tongues, they shall cease; whether there be knowledge, it shall vanish away." Their idea is that when prophecies and knowledge vanish it will be the result of God's specific intervention, while tongues will cease of their own accord. This is based on the voice of the Greek verbs in 1 Corinthians 13:8. The verb *katargeo*, used with "prophecies" and "knowledge," appears in the future passive tense, which is taken to imply God's specific agency and intervention. In contrast, the verb *pauo* which accompanies *glossai* (tongues), is in the future middle, which supposedly suggests that tongues will cease on their own. Church history is then cited by those holding this view as proof that tongues have ceased.

But this interpretation is faulty for two reasons. First, if what has happened in the last seventy-five years can be regarded as Church history, namely widespread evidence of glossolalia, then tongues have not ceased. Even if it be granted that this verse is teaching that tongues will cease of their own accord sometime during Church history and before the Second Coming of Christ, it certainly does not tell us when. To conclude on the basis of this verse that tongues will cease is one thing; to conclude that they definitely ceased during the first few centuries of the Church is quite another.

Second, all such stretching of the Scriptures violates a basic principle of Bible interpretation: It is misleading, even dangerous, to build a major doctrine that tongues are not for today on translation of a single passage. The translation of New Testament Greek in biblical interpretation is important, but to go a step further and read a doctrinal bias into the Greek is clearly wrong and hardly a way to prove that speaking in tongues is not for the Church today.

In summary, speaking in tongues is prayer and praise in known human languages, or prayer and praise in the languages of the Spirit, or both. If more of God's people realized that the exercise of tongues is a part of church history and is not limited to known human languages and linguistic fluency, they might speak in their Spirit-given heavenly languages more readily. No one should be afraid to speak out for the first time. Nor should one despise the *glossa* God has given him. The syllables that may sound like foolish, nonsensical gibberish to the linguistic expert are in fact God-given languages of the Spirit. By the same token, it should not be surprising if someone hears a tongue being spoken and, echoing Acts 2:11, exclaims with astonishment, "He is speaking about the wonderful works of God in a language I recognize and understand!"

Chapter Six

The Evidence of the Baptism

THE EVIDENCE OF THE BAPTISM of the Spirit is speaking in tongues, and although the baptism and tongues are not synonymous, they usually occur at the same time.

In Acts Luke recorded five specific instances when the Holy Spirit was received. These outpourings were a fulfillment of the words of the Old Testament prophets and Jesus.[1] From the accounts of these five occasions, we see the pattern clearly set that speaking in tongues follows the baptism and serves as its evidence.

Pentecost

Without question, the outward sign of the baptism of the Holy Spirit on the day of Pentecost (Acts 2:1–42) was speaking in tongues: "And they were all filled with the Holy Ghost, and began to speak with other tongues" (verse 4). Peter explained to the amazed onlookers that that which they "saw and heard" (verse 33) was evidence that the Spirit of the Lord had been poured out, as had been promised in Joel 2:28–29. Peter then prophesied that this promise of the Holy Spirit, which had been seen and *heard* [tongues], was for everyone (Acts 2:39). The record of Pentecost is sufficient to demonstrate that the evidence of the baptism is speaking in tongues, but God has seen fit to provide four additional witnesses in the book of Acts.

Samaria

The Samaritans (Acts 8:5–25) heard the word of the Lord and believed as a result of Philip's preaching, but they did not receive the gift of the Holy Spirit when they believed. Consequently the church at Jerusalem sent Peter and John, who "laid their hands on them, and they received the Holy Ghost" (verse 17). This passage has been used to dispute the idea that tongues are evidence of the baptism because nowhere in these verses do we read of anyone speaking in tongues. But consider this. In verse 18, we are told that "when Simon [a magician, verse 9] saw that through laying on of the apostles' hands the Holy Ghost was given, he offered them money."

Simon, a man well-acquainted with magic, saw something so unique that he wanted to buy it. We know from the context that he had already witnessed other spectacular miracles in Philip's ministry (verses 6–7), and as a Samaritan he was undoubtedly familiar with the prophetic ministry and Old Testament miracles. Yet when the apostles laid hands on the Samaritans Simon saw something he had never seen before. What did he see? What unusual miracle had escaped his careful investigation of the magical arts? We can reasonably infer that he saw the Samaritans speaking miraculously in other languages.

I am not alone in this view. Even Robert Gromacki, a strong opponent of Pentecostal belief, admits that "although speaking in tongues is not explicitly mentioned in the passage [Acts 8], many commentators believe that the phenomenon occurred then."[2] Among the "many commentators" he mentions in his footnotes are such notables as F.F. Bruce and Merrill C. Tenney.

Paul's Conversion

Shortly after Paul's dramatic conversion on the road to Damascus (Acts 9), "Ananias ... entered into the house; and putting his hands on him said, Brother Saul ... receive thy sight, and be filled with the Holy Ghost" (verse 17). Like Acts 8, this passage has been disputed because tongues are not mentioned in the immediate context. But "Brother Saul" did not take a dim view of speaking in tongues. He wrote some years later, "I thank my God, I speak with tongues more than ye all" (1 Corinthians 14:18). And there is no reason to assume that Paul's experience was different from the other Pentecostal outpourings recorded in the book of Acts. I believe he spoke in tongues the moment he received the Spirit.

The Household of Cornelius

Acts 10:1–48 probably presents the clearest and simplest "proof" that the evidence of the gift of the Spirit is speaking in tongues. After seeing a vision from God, Peter is brought to the house of Cornelius, a Gentile, and understands that he is to preach repentance. We read in verses 45–46 that "they

of the circumcision [the Jews] which believed were astonished, as many as came with Peter, because that on the Gentiles also was poured out the gift of the Holy Ghost. *For they
heard them speak with tongues, and magnify God."* Peter
knew the Gentiles had received the Holy Spirit because they
spoke in tongues. "Then answered Peter . . . (these) have received the Holy Ghost as well as we" (verses 46–47). Later,
when he reported the incident to the disciples in Jerusalem
(Acts 11:1–18), Peter did not have to explain that they had
heard supernatural utterances because it was understood that
the evidence of the baptism was speaking in tongues. Peter
reported, "As I began to speak, the Holy Ghost fell on them
as on us at the beginning" (Acts 11:15). In other words, his
audience knew that Peter's evidence that the Gentiles had
received the baptism was that he heard them speaking in
tongues.

Ephesus

Acts 19:1–7 is the final reference in the book of Acts to the
outpouring of the Spirit. We read in verse 6 that "when Paul
had laid his hands upon them [the disciples in Ephesus], the
Holy Ghost came on them; and they spake with tongues, and
prophesied."

In each of these five references, speaking in tongues as the
evidence of the baptism is either stated or clearly implied.
The well-known *Interpreter's Bible,* an exhaustive commentary on the Scriptures, which is not charismatically oriented,
affirms: "It must be remembered that the author of Acts also
saw in the gift of tongues *proof* that Spirit had been given"
(italics mine).[3] Even an opponent of the charismatic renewal,
Don Hillis, was willing to accept as "technically true" the

statement: "The manifestation of tongues . . . is the normal Scripture pattern wherever a special manifestation is mentioned in connection with the baptism of the Spirit."[4]

Horace Ward makes some lucid remarks in this regard:

> The most controversial issue concerning evidential glossolalia is whether the recipients described in Acts were symbols or patterns. Non-pentecostals generally believe that these cases were representative of certain classes of people, such as Jews, Samaritans, Gentiles, and disciples of John, and that the glossalalic evidence was necessary only for the first recipients within each category. If these were representatives of all the distinct classes of men, would they not prove both the promise and the pattern to be for all? . . . Christ served the Lord's Supper only one time, but Paul recognized His manner as the pattern to be followed universally by the Church. One example is sufficient when God sets it. Are three or four then not sufficient?[5]

The simple and clearly revealed evidence of the baptism of the Spirit is speaking in tongues. Unfortunately this truth has been obscured and complicated by theological debate, even as the simple truth of the gospel has been obscured and complicated by skeptics. For the most part it is those who do not speak in tongues who believe in some other evidence of the baptism of the Spirit. It is as though they are looking to be excused from the pattern.

Further Support for Tongues as Evidence

In addition to the references in the book of Acts to the baptism of the Spirit there are three other biblical arguments that specifically support the view that glossolalia is the evidence of the Spirit. The first, interestingly, comes from what other parts of the Bible *don't* say. Someone may argue: "I can see the pattern in the book of Acts, but if this is so important, why do we read nothing more of this pattern in the epistles?" The virgin birth of Christ serves as an illustration. Only twice in the Gospels and not once in the epistles is the virgin birth of Christ mentioned, yet these two New Testament references have been accepted by evangelicals as sufficient biblical evidence to establish a cardinal doctrine of the Christian faith: Christ was born of a virgin. To argue, "Paul's failure to discuss the virgin birth should cause us to question its validity," is nonsense and illogical. Such reasoning implies that what the epistles do not say is as important as what other portions of the New Testament do say! The silence of the epistles on the evidence of the baptism does not mean that we are to reject categorically the given pattern in the book of Acts. Again I cite Ward:

> It is said that we are arguing from silence when we claim that tongues should logically be assumed in those New Testament cases where they are not specifically reported. Who is arguing from silence? Where is there one occasion where it is specifically stated that they received the Holy Spirit Baptism and did not speak with tongues? In the inspired record, surely a ratio of four to zero sounds more like thunder than like silence.[6]

This reasoning also applies to the multitudes in the book of Acts who were converted, but of whom there is no mention concerning tongues. For example, on the day of Pentecost Peter declared, "The promise [that which had been seen and heard, Acts 2:33] is unto you, and to your children, and to . . . as many as the Lord our God shall call" (Acts 2:39). Though it is not stated that the three thousand new believers spoke in tongues, there is no reason to doubt that they received the

Spirit exactly as Peter and the other disciples had. Would not Peter have expected from the new converts the same evidence of the outpouring of the Spirit that he himself had experienced just moments before? Verse 42 tells us that "they continued steadfastly in the *apostles'* doctrine." My interpretation simply assumes that the usual pattern helps us understand the silence, not vice versa.

The second of these three additional reasons for believing that glossolalia is the evidence of the baptism is that of the nine gifts of the Spirit listed in 1 Corinthians 12, tongues did not appear until the day of Pentecost. Scores of miracles had been performed by Jesus and His disciples and had been witnessed by multitudes *before* Pentecost, but the distinguishing miracle of Acts 2 was speaking in other tongues. Seven of the nine gifts in 1 Corinthians 12 are never reported in the New Testament as manifestations of the baptism. Only tongues and prophecy are found in that context, and prophecy occurs but once (Acts 19:6).

The third reason is that the gifts of tongues and interpretation of tongues are the only two gifts of the Spirit not manifested under the Old Covenant. The other gifts, as well as the infilling of the Spirit, were not foreign to the Old Testament. As evidence of the *New* Covenant, the Spirit of God brought a *new* sign. In 1 Corinthians 14:21 we read: "In the law it is written, With men of other tongues and other lips will I speak unto this people." Under the inspiration of the Holy Spirit, Paul applies this Old Testament passage directly to glossolalia. It is significant that this prophetic portion (Isaiah 28:11–12) points to the giving of the New Covenant. Centuries before the birth of Christ, Isaiah predicted that "other tongues," an unusual and unique miracle, would signify the establishment of the New Covenant.

In view of the biblical evidence offered, it is not difficult to accept speaking in tongues as the sign of the baptism of the Holy Spirit. Don Basham writes, "Those who ask the question, 'Do I *have* to speak in tongues?' make it sound as if they are being asked to swallow an unpleasant dose of medicine. Their question indicates they believe tongues is something to be endured rather than enjoyed! Speaking in tongues is a blessed experience! It is a joy and privilege to be able to communicate with the Lord in this new and exciting manner. Someone has rightly said, 'You don't have to, you *get* to!' Or as Dr. David du Plessis comments, 'You don't have to, but you will.' "[7]

The question has been frequently asked, "You mean if I have not spoken in tongues, then I do not have the baptism of the Holy Spirit?"

Speaking in tongues is the outward sign of a deep, inner work of the Spirit. One person cannot look into the heart of another and determine whether or not that individual is saved. Similarly, one cannot look into a person's heart and determine without question that he or she has or has not received the baptism of the Holy Spirit. Yet in both cases, we can expect fruit. The evidence of salvation is the fruit of the Spirit. The evidence of the baptism is the charismata of the Spirit, initiated by speaking in other tongues. Speaking in tongues, like the fruit of the Spirit, is the "firstfruits" of an inner work, not merely for God's sake, but for man's.

You may believe that you have received the baptism of the Holy Spirit, and you may have. But if you do not speak in tongues, then in my view you have no real evidence that you have indeed experienced the Pentecostal outpouring. If you have received the baptism of the Spirit, you can and *should* speak in other tongues. And if you are genuinely open to the Lord in this area, you *will*.

Chapter Seven

Are Tongues for Everyone?

In 1 CORINTHIANS 12:30 Paul asks, "Have all the gifts of healing? do all speak with tongues?" Those who have been opposed to speaking in tongues or who have been hesitant to become involved in the phenomenon have quoted this text in self-defense. But to do so is to misunderstand the context of the verse. In this chapter the apostle Paul is not discussing the private use of tongues, which I feel should be exercised regularly by every believer to supplement his devotional life. Instead, Paul is talking about the ministry of tongues to the whole church. In other words, not everyone will have the *public* ministry of tongues.

This is shown by the immediate context. For example, in verse 28 Paul mentions the ministry of "helps," yet helping others is certainly not to be the exclusive right of a select few who may have the gift. Though some have a special ministry

67

in this regard, every servant of the Lord is expected to be faithful and helpful. Another gift Paul mentions is that of "teacher." Once again, though some do have the special ministry gift of teaching, everyone should be able to teach and share the basics of the gospel message (see Hebrews 5:12).

This distinction is further clarified by what Paul writes about prophecy. Expecting the answer no, he asks, "Are *all* prophets?" (1 Corinthians 12:29), while on the other hand he teaches that "ye may *all* prophesy" (1 Corinthians 14:31). The ability to prophesy occasionally does not make one a prophet. So it is with tongues. While some have the special gift of ministering in tongues in a public meeting, everyone should be exercising the gift of tongues in his private communion with the Lord.

For this reason Paul writes a seemingly contradictory statement in 1 Corinthians 14:5: "I would that ye *all* spake with tongues." We must remember that Paul wrote these things under the inspiration of the Holy Spirit and as "commandments of the Lord" (verse 37). Thus, because this verse is the inspired Word of God and not just Paul's personal opinion, we can assume it represents the very desire of the Spirit of the Lord. God Himself is telling us in His Word, "I would that you *all* spake with tongues."

It should also be pointed out that this Greek word translated "would" (I *would* that ye ...) expresses more than a mere wish. In fact, this same word is used in 1 Timothy 2:4 where we read that the Lord "*will* have all men to be saved, and to come unto the knowledge of the truth."

Paul also says in 1 Corinthians 14:5 that it is better to prophesy than to speak in tongues. It is better because the ministry of prophecy benefits the entire Church, while speaking in tongues, unless there is an interpreter, benefits only the individual. But it is wrong to conclude on the basis of this verse that we do not need tongues. Similarly, in 1 Corinthians 7, Paul indicates that for the sake of the ministry it is better to remain unmarried. But this does not mean we are to avoid or despise marriage. We should have all spiritual blessings, both small and large, in heavenly places in Christ Jesus.

That the Pentecostal experience is for everyone is indicated in Acts 2:17: "And it shall come to pass in the last days, saith God, I will pour out of my Spirit upon *all flesh.*" The universality of the baptism of the Spirit is further explained in Peter's sermon in this same chapter. In verses 32 and 33 Peter declares, "This Jesus hath God raised up, whereof we all are witnesses. Therefore being by the right hand of God exalted, and having received of the Father the *promise* of the Holy Ghost, he hath shed forth this, which ye now *see* and *hear.*" The word *promise* is a key to understanding this passage. Peter indicated that the "promise of the Holy Ghost" could be seen and heard. It was seen in that the disciples were acting like drunken men; it was heard in that they were all speaking with other tongues. "He [Jesus] hath shed forth this [the promise of the Holy Spirit] which ye now *see* and *hear.*"

All this is deeply significant when we study Peter's next mention of "the promise." After the multitude cried out for salvation Peter said to them, "Repent, and be baptized every one of you in the name of Jesus Christ for the remission of sins, and ye shall receive the gift of the Holy Ghost. For *the promise* [which they had *seen* and *heard*] is unto you, and to your children, and to *all* that are afar off, *even as many as the Lord our God shall call*" (verses 38–39). The promise of the

Holy Spirit—the baptism of the Holy Spirit evidenced by speaking in other tongues (things seen and heard)—is for as many as the Lord our God shall call! The baptism of the Holy Spirit accompanied by speaking in tongues is indeed for everyone!

Chapter Eight

Reasons for Speaking in Tongues

WHAT GOOD IS THERE in speaking in other tongues? The answer implied by this common question is, Not much. Charismatics are repeatedly reminded that speaking in tongues is the least of the gifts, and because its spiritual value is minimal, there is no point in bothering with it. Better to spend time pursuing more important things, like the fruits of the Spirit—love and peace, for instance.

But the Bible reveals that glossolalia is not merely emotional gibberish reserved only for those who are so selfishly inclined to edify themselves. On the contrary, speaking in tongues is a powerful and versatile tool in the hands of the one possessing the gift.

Tongues Are a Sign

One important aspect of speaking in tongues is its use as a "sign." A sign is something that signifies; it is an identifying mark or token. Speaking in tongues is an identifying mark in several ways.

First, tongues were a sign to Israel of the New Covenant. Isaiah predicted that God would speak to Israel "with stammering lips and another tongue" (Isaiah 28:11). Although this passage certainly had other implications in the history of Israel, Paul applied this passage directly to the New Testament gift of tongues. He wrote: "In the law it is written, With men of other tongues and other lips will I speak unto this people. . . . Wherefore *tongues are for a sign*" (1 Corinthians 14:21–22). Israel could know that the New Covenant, the dispensation of rest and refreshing (Isaiah 28:12; Acts 3:19), had been initiated through the outpouring of the Spirit signified by speaking in other tongues.

On the day of Pentecost "there were dwelling at Jerusalem Jews, devout men, out of every nation under heaven" (Acts 2:5). Multitudes from around the world had made the pilgrimage to the Holy Land to celebrate the feast of Pentecost. When the Holy Spirit was poured out upon the disciples in the Upper Room, "this was noised abroad. . . . And they [the Jews in Jerusalem] were all amazed, and were in doubt, saying one to another, What meaneth this?" (Acts 2:6, 12). Peter was quick to respond: Speaking in tongues and all this commotion is a fulfillment of that which was spoken by the prophet Joel. This is a sign to you of the giving of the Holy Spirit and the beginning of a new era—the last days. Repent, therefore, and the times of refreshing promised by Isaiah the prophet will come from the presence of the Lord (Acts 2:16–17; 3:19, paraphrased). Speaking in tongues—an unprecedented, confounding, amazing, and marvelous event (Acts 2:6–7)—was a sign to Israel of the outpouring of the Holy Spirit and the beginning of the age of the New Covenant.

Second, tongues are a sign of the resurrection and ascension of Christ. Peter preached, "This Jesus hath God raised up, whereof we all are witnesses. Therefore, being by the right hand of God exalted, and having received of the Father the promise of the Holy Ghost, he hath shed forth this, which ye now *see and hear* [namely, speaking in tongues, tongues of fire, and the mighty rushing wind]" (Acts 2:32–33).

Third, tongues are a sign of the baptism of the Spirit. I have already discussed at length in Chapter 6 that speaking in tongues is the evidence of the baptism of the Holy Spirit. This alone, if accepted as biblical truth, is sufficient reason to stress the importance of speaking in tongues, not as an end in itself, but as a sign of the outpouring of the Spirit. "On the Gentiles also was poured out the gift of the Holy Ghost. *For they heard them speak with tongues,* and magnify God" (Acts 10:45–46).

Fourth, speaking in tongues is also a sign of believers: "And these *signs* shall follow them that *believe.*" Among other things, those who believe "shall speak with new tongues" (Mark 16:17).

Finally, tongues are a sign to unbelievers. Tongues are identified in Mark 16 as a sign that should follow those who believe. This also implies that this powerful utterance gift can be a dramatic testimony to unbelievers, especially when the languages are recognized. It is not surprising that such a miracle at Pentecost resulted in the conversion of souls.

When tongues are not understood, however, they may be misunderstood! On the day of Pentecost not everyone marveled over the heavenly utterances. "Others mocking said, These men are full of new wine" (Acts 2:13). When those who doubt it are present, the manifestation of tongues can be met by a mixed response. Paul refers to this in 1 Corinthians 14:22–23: "Wherefore tongues are for a sign [something obscure], not to them that believe, but to them that believe not. . . . If therefore the whole church be come together into one place, and all speak with tongues, and there come in those that are unlearned, or unbelievers, will they not say that ye are mad?" This is precisely what happened on the day of Pentecost. The reaction of the crowd was not entirely favorable.

Krister Stendahl, a preeminent New Testament scholar, explains 1 Corinthians 14:22 as follows· "The key to the problem is what Paul means by 'sign.' I suggest that the word 'sign' had a negative connotation for Paul [in this verse]. It refers to a 'mere sign,' a sign that does not lead to faith but to non-hearing, to the hardening of unbelief (verse 21)."[1] Thus, to unbelievers "tongues are for a sign," a sign that may or may not be understood. Sometimes tongues-speaking is met by a positive response, especially when the languages are recognized, and other times by a negative and critical response, as indicated here and in Acts 2.

The Importance of Tongues in the Life of the Believer

There are several reasons why tongues are important to the believer personally. The first is this: "He that speaketh in an unknown tongue edifieth himself" (1 Corinthians 14:4). Speaking in tongues, like so many other aspects of the Christian life, brings personal edification. Some discredit tongues on the premise that personal edification is selfish. Such reasoning is blind. Would the same person who opposes tongues refuse to attend church? Pray for himself? Seek personal counsel? Even Jesus prayed for Himself, and we would not dare accuse Him of being selfish. Speaking in tongues is a source of personal encouragement and edification for "build ing up yourselves on your most holy faith, praying in the Holy Ghost" (Jude 20).

Second, tongues are also necessary for the edification of the Church. Paul indicated that when tongues are interpreted, the spiritual influence on the Church is similar to the impact of prophetic utterance. "Greater is he that prophesieth than he that speaketh with tongues, *except he interpret*, that the church may receive edifying" (1 Corinthians 14:5).

Third, tongues are for prayer. "He that speaketh in an unknown tongue speaketh not unto men, but unto God" (1 Corinthians 14:2). Prayer is speaking to God. In 1 Corinthians 14:14–15 Paul indicates that he himself prayed in tongues, and he suggests that our prayers may be spoken in the language we understand—"I will pray with the understanding"—or in languages we do not understand—"if I pray in an unknown tongue, my spirit prayeth, but my understanding is unfruitful."

Such prayer in the Spirit is accurate and effective. "We know not what we should pray for as we ought: but the Spirit . . . maketh intercession for the saints according to the will of God" (Romans 8:26–27). This passage in Romans is not a reference to speaking in tongues, *per se*, but the application to prayer in the Spirit is undeniable. Only the Spirit's prayers are in perfect harmony with the will of God, whether He intercedes for us (Romans 8:26), or through us (1 Corinthians 14:2).

Such prayer in the Spirit is also confidental. This applies to those times when we are praying in the Spirit for the needs of others. When we are praying in tongues alone or in public, the Holy Spirit is able to pinpoint personal needs without violating an individual's privacy.

Fourth, tongues are for worship. Kevin Ranaghan writes,

"If tongues serve any purpose at all, it is not in the realm of petition or of edification or of public prayer that we will find the fundamental, essential and ultimate 'use' of this gift. It is praise!"[2] In 1 Corinthians 14:15–17 Paul refers to singing, blessing, and offering thanksgiving in the Spirit. On the day of Pentecost, the acclamation of the multitudes was, "We do hear them speak in our tongues the wonderful works of God." Worship and praise! And when Cornelius and his household received the outpouring of the Spirit, they not only spoke with new tongues, they magnified God (Acts 10:46).

Finally, speaking in tongues is a testimony of a person's willingness for God to control his entire being. "Behold, we put bits in the horses' mouths, that they may obey us; and we turn about their whole body. Behold also the ships, which though they be so great, and are driven of fierce winds, yet are they turned about with a very small helm. . . . Even so the *tongue* is a little member, and boasteth great things. Behold, how great a matter a little fire kindleth! And the tongue is a fire, a world of iniquity: so is the tongue among our members, that it defileth the whole body. . . . The tongue can *no man tame*" (James 3:3–8).

In the light of these words it is interesting that speaking in tongues is so opposed—even by some who desire to receive the baptism in the Holy Spirit. "I will receive any gift but tongues. Tongues are meaningless gibberish. Do I have to speak in tongues?"

The resistance to this precious but peculiar gift is unending. Why? When the Lord controls the tongue, He controls the whole body. Could it be that a willingness to speak in tongues is a kind of ultimate affirmation of the Lordship of Christ?

It is also interesting to relate this to the matter of witnessing. "Ye shall receive power, after that the Holy Ghost is come upon you: and ye shall be witnesses unto me" (Acts 1:8). Howard Ervin writes, "Inasmuch as the human faculty preeminently used in witnessing is the power of speech, it need come as no surprise, nor should it jar our aesthetic sense of propriety, that on the day of Pentecost the Spirit's fullness was manifest in supernatural utterance."[3]

Chapter Nine

Tongues and Emotionalism

THE WORD OF GOD commands, "Forbid not to speak with tongues," or according to the Greek text, "Quit forbidding to speak in tongues" (1 Corinthians 14:39). Yet in spite of the clear scriptural injunction, there are Christians today who continue to forbid speaking in tongues, directly or indirectly. Without giving much careful thought to what they are saying, certain well-meaning believers warn us of three awful dangers of speaking in tongues: "It is emotionalism! It is of the devil! It is divisive!" My purpose is to demonstrate that these objections are invalid. These next three chapters will deal with each of these objections.

Are Tongues Just Emotionalism?

In answer to those who complain that speaking in tongues is an emotional experience, I reply, "In some cases, you're right!" Those of us who speak in tongues have nothing to hide when it comes to our emotional experiences in the Spirit. Certainly, excessive emotionalism can be offensive, but I would rather that God's people risk emotional excess than suffer the disease of spiritual and emotional insensitivity. As one charismatic brother wrote, "There's nothing biblical about spiritual deadness."[1] Our Lord Himself solemnly warned us of the consequences of lukewarm Christianity (Revelation 3:15–16).

God created man an emotional being. The Bible is filled with testimonies of emotional experiences. Even God Himself is described as having emotions. Shouldn't we be careful then not to criticize—carelessly or otherwise—an emotional expression of prayer, praise, and worship? I suggest that resistance to emotional Christianity is merely the reflection of the source of all sin—pride. Human beings do not want to be seen doing "foolish things." Take King David's wife Michal, for example. When she saw her dignified husband making a "fool" of himself by dancing with joy in the streets of Jerusalem, "she despised him in her heart" (1 Chronicles 15:29).

People can become carried away emotionally at a sporting event and we think little of it; in fact, the success of a sporting contest is often measured by its level of excitement and emotional appeal. But someone who gets emotional about God is labeled "irreverent" or "a fanatic."

Like the Pharisees in the days of Christ, religious people still seem to want to take the joy out of our relationship with the Lord. When Jesus entered Jerusalem in triumph, His followers were shouting, "Blessed be the King that cometh in the name of the Lord!" (Luke 19:38). The Pharisees hissed, "Master, rebuke thy disciples" (verse 39). Tragically, these same words are being spoken or implied in many of our churches today. Emotionalism as a response to faith is not wrong. Resistance to emotionalism is wrong.

Some do not object to emotional responses to God, but do object to speaking in tongues because it seems to make people lose control of themselves and do strange things. "Holyroller" is not a title that has been conferred with affection. This kind of thinking, however, indicates a misconception of tongues. Tongues and the accompanying manifestations of the Spirit will always appear peculiar to the outsider. Indeed, ever since the day of Pentecost speaking in tongues has been misunderstood. That the Pentecostal experience has been abused I cannot deny, but abuse is no reason to reject the truth of Scripture.

Speaking in tongues need not be viewed as a frightening and uncontrolled experience. Speaking in tongues is, writes Larry Christensen, "as the Bible so accurately puts it, simply 'a speaking.' It has the same emotional potential (and the same possibility of self-control) as speech or prayer in one's native tongue."[2] Don Basham adds, "The idea that one has to . . . go into a trance or 'lose control' in order to receive the Holy Spirit or manifest His gifts is simply not true. While emotional excesses may be indulged in by certain fringe groups, the fact is that most people receiving the baptism of the Holy Spirit today receive it among people who worship in churches similar to their own and whose religious backgrounds are compatible with theirs."[3]

By its very nature speaking in tongues does not have to be accompanied by an emotional experience. Yet at times it is, and unless this emotional response is consistently excessive, it should be recognized and accepted as biblically sound.

Tongues and Psychology

Another objection to speaking in tongues, related to emotionalism, involves the psychological implications of glossolalia. Donald Burdick, author of *Tongues: To Speak or Not to Speak*, describes glossolalia as "a phenomenon bordering on the psychopathic."[4] Such criticism denies that tongues-speaking is a legitimate biblical experience. Those who analyze and reject tongues from a psychological point of view are not using the Bible as their primary reference or standard of truth.

Speaking with Tongues, by Stuart Bergsma, raises another objection. He confidently affirms that "modern glossolalia is in an entirely different category from Pentecost glossolalia and true glossolalia in the gospel age and Pauline age."[5] I wonder how Bergsma can be so sure—considering he wasn't present with first-century Christians to analyze the psychology of speaking in tongues! I fear what conclusions would be drawn if Paul's spiritual experiences (supernatural conversion, tongues, miracles, the third heaven) were subjected to the scrutiny of a modern psychiatrist. Bergsma goes so far as to group modern glossolalia with "the ouija board craze," "spiritualistic seances in the dark," and "mind reading."[6] This kind of evaluation skirts the clear biblical command, "Forbid not to speak with tongues." In a similar treatise on the psychology of tongues entitled "Psychological Observations," John Kildahl likewise disregards the biblical injunction.[7]

All Christians, not just those who speak in tongues, have at one time or another been labeled "psychologically maladjusted." But Paul's words in 1 Corinthians 1:27 counter this diagnosis: "But God hath chosen the foolish things of the world to confound the wise. . . ." I am also happy to report the psychological finding that "recent studies of the Pentecostal experience rid us of one of the old mythical bugaboos which has long plagued the Pentecostal movement. Pentecostals are not less healthy mentally than are other Christians."[8]

Howard Ervin writes, "The commonplace assumption that biblical *glossolalia* is the result of pathological emotional states simply ignores the fact that they are a supernatural manifestation of the Holy Spirit. To ascribe them to the abnormal working of a damaged psyche is to impugn the veracity of the biblical records, to say nothing of the integrity of the multiplied thousands of tongue-speaking Christians whose emotional health is equal if not superior, to that of their critics."[9]

Chapter Ten

Speaking in Tongues Is Not From the Devil

CHRISTIANS OFTEN HESITATE to ask for the baptism of the Spirit, fearing they might encounter a demon or even come under the influence of Satan. Non-Pentecostals have successfully detoured many believers by using these scare tactics, but have apparently not stopped to consider that their contention is not biblical. Though this is a common anti-charismatic argument held by numerous Bible-believing Christians, no such warning is found in the Bible.

This objection to speaking in tongues is the logical conclusion to the premise that speaking in tongues is not for today. If a person firmly believes that glossolalia is not to be practiced by the Church today, he must explain why so many are speaking in tongues in spite of his theological position. If the phenomenon is a supernatural experience, and if it is not from God, the only other possible source, he reasons, is Satan himself.

Granted, the supernatural gifts of the Spirit have been misused and abused, and counterfeit "tongues" do occur outside of Christianity. But to wave danger flags in these areas is to avoid the issue: Glossolalia is a New Testament gift. For this reason every Christian must examine, accept, and appreciate the gift, even if he does not understand it, even if it's abused, even if it's counterfeited in other religions. There are at least three sound reasons for rejecting the view that tongues have a demonic origin.

First, in Luke 11 Jesus Himself promises that if any of His children ask for the Holy Spirit, He will not give them a demon. "If a son shall ask bread of . . . a father, will he give him a stone? or if he ask a fish, will he . . . give him a serpent? Or if he shall ask an egg, will he offer him a scorpion?" (Luke 11:11–12). "Serpent" and "scorpion" are recognized symbols of the devil and hell. In the same chapter in Luke's Gospel Jesus commented, "I give unto you power to tread on serpents and scorpions, and over all the power of the enemy" (Luke 10:19). Instead of slipping us serpents and scorpions, our heavenly Father will "give the Holy Spirit to them that ask him" (Luke 11:13). Almost in anticipation of the contemporary objections to speaking in tongues, Jesus absolutely rules out any possibility of demonic intervention if a believer requests the Holy Spirit.

To argue that these verses apply dispensationally to Israel is not a primary concern. If these verses do refer to Israel under an old covenant relationship, and if in that relationship the Father guarantees the gift of the Spirit to those who ask, how much more firm His promise of the Spirit must be to us who are living in the New Testament age following the experience of Pentecost!

In the back of the popular gospel tract, *The Four Spiritual Laws,* the Christian witness is instructed to ask the one who has just received Christ, "Where is Jesus now?" The expected response is, "In my heart." "How do you know He is there?" the witness pursues. "Because He said He would come in if I asked Him to," the new Christian answers.

This teaching on the assurance of salvation is based on the promise of Christ. His Word is as pure as His character. If Jesus said it, we should believe it. Who could imagine anyone warning a new convert, "Now if you are not sincere, if you are not genuine, if you are not careful, you may receive a demon when you ask for Christ to come into your heart." Such a thought borders on blasphemy! Yet certain Christians have no qualms about warning fellow believers that if they get involved in the "Holy Spirit movement" they may receive a demon instead of the Spirit. Perhaps the devil is not so much at work among those who are earnestly seeking the baptism of the Spirit and speaking in tongues as he is deviously responsible for all the fear that keeps believers from desiring the Pentecostal experience.

The second reason we may reject the theory of the demonic origin of tongues is that the apostle Paul warns us of no such connection. No other book in the New Testament discusses glossolalia and the other supernatural charismata more thoroughly than 1 Corinthians, and probably no other church has ever had more problems with tongues than the church at Corinth. Yet in spite of all their Pentecostal excess, Paul never once warns the Corinthians of "devil-danger" in relation to speaking in tongues. Certainly the gift was misunderstood and abused, but the cure for the ailments of that church was not avoiding the gifts out of fear of demons. The remedy was teaching, spiritual growth, and the crucifixion of the flesh.

If devil-danger were so likely, the Holy Spirit would surely have inspired Paul to warn the Corinthians against it. Of all the places in the Bible where we might expect to see this kind of warning, 1 Corinthians is the place. Yet we do not find even a suggestion along these lines anywhere in the text of this epistle.

The greatest reason of all not to attribute tongues to the devil is found in Matthew 12:22–37 where Jesus speaks of blasphemy against the Holy Spirit. This ultimate, unpardonable sin is commonly defined as persistent rejection of the Holy Spirit's conviction. A careful look at Scripture gives us an even more precise idea of the nature of this sin.

Jesus had just cast a demon out of a blind and dumb man and the Pharisees reacted by giving credit for the expulsion to Satan. "This fellow doth not cast out devils, but by Beelzebub the prince of devils," they chided (Matthew 12:24). In other words, they said that Jesus cast out devils by the power of Satan. It was in response to this accusation that Christ addressed His remarks on the sin of blasphemy against the Holy Spirit—"Because they said, He hath an unclean spirit" (Mark 3:30) when in fact He was ministering under the anointing of the Holy Spirit. This shows us that the sin Christ so solemnly warned against was attributing the works of the Holy Spirit to the devil.

In view of these words of Christ, careful thought should be given to attributing tongues—clearly associated in the Bible with the outpouring of the Holy Spirit—to an unclean spirit. As A. T. Robertson writes in his commentary on Matthew 12, "People often ask if they can commit the unpardonable sin.

Probably some do who ridicule the manifest work of God's Spirit in men's lives and attribute the Spirit's work to the devil."[1]

Don Basham has considered this same grave implication.

> To blaspheme against the Holy Spirit is to deliberately proclaim the power of God to be the power of Satan. It is to define the Holy Spirit's power as demonic power; it is to "speak against the Holy Spirit" by deliberately accusing one anointed by the Holy Spirit of being under the control of Satan. We could even say that one who blasphemes against the Holy Spirit insinuates that God is Satan or Satan is God.[2]

It is not my purpose to accuse any opponents of the charismatic renewal of blasphemy against the Holy Spirit. But when someone takes the liberty of identifying Pentecostal experiences with the work of the devil, I will take the liberty to point out the serious implication of that accusation.

The cry of devil-danger is not a valid biblical objection to speaking in tongues. It is an emotionally loaded appeal from the very ones who accuse Pentecostals of being emotional.

Chapter Eleven

The Divisiveness of Tongues

"THE CHARISMATIC MOVEMENT is divisive. Speaking in tongues splits churches. Pentecostals think they are super-spiritual because of their special experiences. Charismatics have driven a wedge between themselves and other Christians."

Do these criticisms sound familiar? Non-charismatics have rejected the present move of the Spirit because, among other things, it supposedly causes division, and anything that causes division has to be wrong—or does it?

The Bible teaches that divisive elements in the church can be wrong (1 Corinthians), and we are commanded to endeavor to "keep the unity of the Spirit in the bond of peace" (Ephesians 4:3). On the other hand, we are never told to reject or compromise truth simply because it may create a division by making someone nervous.

Jesus did not hesitate to make the Pharisees nervous, even though His love for them was immeasurable. Peter made the Jews nervous when on the day of Pentecost he boldly declared, "This is that which was spoken by the prophet

Joel." With all due respect for divinely ordained authority, Paul made the Roman officials nervous when he preached an uncompromising gospel. Martin Luther made the Roman Catholic hierarchy nervous when he exposed corruption in the ecclesiastical system and spoke openly of salvation by grace alone. William Carey, the father of modern missions, made his denomination nervous when he violated theological tradition and carried the salvation message to the desperate multitudes in India.

The blood-stained graves of countless Christians punctuate the words of Jesus: "Think not that I am come to send peace on earth: I came not to send peace, but a sword" (see Matthew 10:34–39). Thompson, in his *Chain Reference Bible*, gives simple but penetrating subtitles to these verses: "Christ the Divider" and "The Conflict of Truth."

Division can originate from one or both of two sources. The first has its roots in the pride of man and grieves the Holy Spirit; the second is noble and is the consequence of the sword of truth. I believe that the primary source of the divisions over charismatic teaching originates from the latter of these.

Thomas Smail writes: "The first charismatic renewal, when the Man filled with the Spirit [Jesus] was set loose in mighty deed throughout Galilee, *was inevitably and deeply divisive.* By its sheer reality and authenticity, by its bringing the issues of the kingdom out of their theological remoteness and manifesting the glory of God in deeds done to neighbors on the lakeside and in the market place, a situation was created *where neutrality towards it* became impossible" (italics mine).[1] If the charismatic renewal is of man, it should be rejected out of hand. But if it is of God we must ask ourselves who is really causing the divisions—those who hold to the truth, or those who oppose it.

Speaking in tongues is never divisive; division is caused by people—people who refuse or abuse tongues. Dick Dugan writes, "As to divisions and splits, which surely are to be deplored, neither speaking in tongues nor disallowing tongues has ever split any body of believers. It is not the gifts that divide, but carnality—and that on both sides of the issue."[2] Even for Paul, tongues were not a problem; the Corinthians were.

Pentecostals have not always used wisdom in the exercise of the gifts, nor has their sharing with others always been with kindness and consideration. Blunders have been made, and not infrequently. But again, misuse is not an excuse. Regardless of how tongues are being used or abused we should keep our attention focused on the Word, not on the person who has misapplied or misunderstood the Word. The attitudes and actions of misguided saints should never deter us from understanding and appreciating what God has promised in the Bible.

True, speaking in tongues has resulted in bitter misunderstanding. At the same time, as James Logan points out, the "institutional church by its conservative defensiveness toward something new can create a climate of distrust, encouraging the new charismatic to expect alienation and martyrdom."[3] Charismatics have had their share of shortcomings, but they are not always the ones to blame.

Some have tried to avoid these people-problems by suggesting that the controversy is rooted in Pentecostal theology, which ostensibly creates two levels of Christians: those who have received the fullness of the Spirit and those who have not. But I reply that all theological differences, Pentecostal or not, tend to create two levels of Christians: those who believe in a particular doctrine and those who do not. If we reject charismatics on this basis alone we are forced to reject everyone who disagrees with us on anything. Avoiding the people-problems does not resolve the conflicts.

Satan always opposes the truth and power of God viciously. In a certain sense, Christianity is more divided (hundreds of denominations and splinter groups) than any other religion in the world. Yet this sad fact is actually a "proof" for the validity of Christianity. The fractured Church is evidence that Satan has leveled his artillery at the truth. The devil is not nearly so active when men are blinded by religious delusions. Why should he bother with a man who is already deceived? Similarly, the bitter opposition to the charismatic renewal suggests that there is vital truth at the core of the revival and Satan is opposing it. When people discover the limitless power of the baptism of the Spirit, Satan adamantly resists them.

In summary, the turmoil over speaking in tongues and the charismatic renewal should not be blamed on Pentecostal doctrine, nor is it the fault of misdirected tongues-speakers. The divisions are just as much the fault of those who resist what God is trying to say to the Church, and Satan, of course, is feeding the fires.

How tragic that the Church of the Lord Jesus Christ is so at odds over the ministry of the Spirit—the very Spirit whose purpose is to bring unity to the members of the Body! Paul once wrote to a church beset by charismatic controversy, "Though I speak with the tongues of men and of angels," and even if I do not speak with tongues of men and of angels, "and have not love," it profits me nothing. "The way for both those with and those without the experience to keep the phenomenon in perspective," writes Watson Mills, "is neither to forbid nor force tongues, but rather to exercise mutual tolerance, understanding and love."[4]

Chapter Twelve

Are Charismatics Experience-Oriented?

OFTEN CHARISMATICS are accused of endorsing the baptism of the Spirit purely because they believe they have experienced it. We are told, "You are just arguing from experience," which gives non-charismatics, who haven't encountered the Spirit, a feeling of biblical certainty. They remind charismatics that the Bible alone, not an experience, is our only sure foundation, a point that no charismatic would argue with! In fact, as we have already seen, the Bible is the greatest platform from which to argue the charismatic position.

Where then does experience fit in all of this? Is it a valid consideration for either side of the debate?

· The appearance of tongues, charismatic gifts, and miracles in the New Testament cannot be questioned. It is their meaning today that is debated. To say that Pentecostal theology is experience-centered and therefore not biblical is to argue in principle that non-Pentecostal doctrine is also experience-centered and not biblical. Why? Pentecostals understand the Bible on the basis of Pentecostal experience; because they speak in tongues, they believe that tongues are for today. In contrast, non-Pentecostals understand the Bible on the basis of their non-Pentecostal experience; because they do not speak in tongues, they believe that tongues are not for today. The experience of tongues is the starting point for understanding the gifts for the one, while an experience devoid of tongues is the starting point for the other. To a certain extent, both positions start from experience. And actually, Pentecostals have less difficulty explaining their experience by the Word of God than non-Pentecostals have explaining them away.

No Christian apologist would deny the importance of experience. The fourth of the *Four Spiritual Laws* emphasizes the necessity of a personal encounter with Christ. It is not enough just to believe; even the devils do that (James 2:19). A person must accept Christ as his personal Savior, and experience Him. It takes a revelation of the Spirit, an "experience," if we may use the term in this way, to understand fully the things of God. "Faith cometh by hearing, and hearing by the word of God," but unless the divine Teacher quickens faith experientially, no amount of hearing will ever save the soul.

Christians are quick to point out that the Bible can never be fully understood apart from the experience of repentance and rebirth. Similarly, Pentecostals contend that tongues and the other gifts of the Spirit can never be fully understood until after one has experienced the baptism of the Spirit. This does not elevate the experience above the Bible. Like Paul's dramatic conversion, every experience must be judged by the

Word of God; but if the experience is biblical, it must not be rejected.

Robert K. Johnston in *Christianity Today* states:

> To stress one's experience, which is an experience of the Spirit, is not, according to evangelicals, to ignore the Word as manifest both in Scripture and in Christ himself. Indeed, to do so would be foolish, for it would result in a formless mysticism. Word and Spirit must be joined together in *any* Christian theology. What is being increasingly attempted today is a reversal of the Reformer's *approach* to the Christian faith. Evangelicals are suggesting that theology must travel from Spirit to Word, not from Word to Spirit, the pattern of our heritage.[1]

On the one hand, the Bible governs *absolutely* our experiences; but on the other hand, our experiences help us comprehend the Word. Pentecostal theology cannot be dismissed simply because it stresses experience any more than fundamentalism can be dismissed because it grew out of a need to stress experience in the face of dead orthodoxy.

Three times in the book of Acts Paul gives a testimony, and each time his conversion *experience* is the focal point. But what gives his testimony authority is its correlation with the Scriptures. "I was not disobedient unto the heavenly vision," Paul proclaimed (Acts 26:19). How many non-charismatics would accept this kind of testimony today? Yet Paul's vision was not mere mysticism, because it was in the scheme of the prophets. He adds: "I continue... saying none other things than those which the prophets and Moses did say should come" (Acts 26:22). Similarly, charismatics share their experiences as a valid and vital feature of New Testament revelation.

On the day of Pentecost, after the disciples had been ridiculed for speaking in tongues, Peter went directly to the Scriptures: "This is that which was spoken by the prophet Joel" (Acts 2:16). Nearly two thousand years later the Pentecostal defense has not changed: This is that spoken of by the Scriptures.

One can argue about the meaning of the Bible, the meaning of charismatic teaching and practice, or that charismatics are experience-oriented. But no one can deny that speaking in tongues and other charismatic manifestations are part of New Testament truth. If the Pentecostal is guilty of arguing from his experience, the non-Pentecostal is equally guilty, if I may say so, because he argues from his lack of experience.

Chapter Thirteen

The Spiritual Gifts in Church History

THEOLOGIANS HAVE LONG debated the significance of supernatural gifts of the Spirit in Church history. While some argue that the "sign gifts" disappeared shortly after the death of the apostles, others disagree, pointing to the appearance of the gifts throughout the centuries.

In this latter vein, Williams and Waldvogel write:

> Pentecostalism as an organized movement is a phenomenon of the twentieth century, but as a force it derives from many centuries of Christian tradition. The common religious experience of individuals and groups throughout history demonstrates a shared and similar working of one Spirit.[1]

Since the Church has generally disregarded this testimony—because of the fanaticism or unorthodoxy of groups assuming the practice—it has taught that tongues at Pentecost were a supernatural gift of foreign languages for apostolic evangelism in the first century Church alone. In spite of this belief, we will see that the use of tongues as a language of prayer and praise has indeed persisted through the history of the Church.

The Charismata in the Second Century

The attitudes and doctrinal perceptions of the early Church concerning the charismata (or *pneumatika*, spiritual or supernatural things) were not clearly defined until the issue became schismatic with the rise of the Montanists. The prominence of miracles in the early Church seems to have waned in comparison with Acts, and there are but scattered references among the early Fathers. Nevertheless, certain citations do substantiate the general acceptance of supernatural occurrences. Lebreton observes:

> All our efforts nowadays are directed to obtaining the recognition of a fact (a cure, resurrection, or prophecy) as supernatural; in the second century, this point was not the most difficult to get recognized. People found no great difficulty in allowing an activity superior to that of natural agents, but the whole problem was to discern the origin of these supernatural activities.[2]

In other words, the Church in the second century did not argue whether or not miracles occurred, but whether their source was God or the devil. That miracles happened was assumed.

Justin Martyr, in his *Apology* addressed to the Roman emperor, wrote:

> For numberless demoniacs throughout the whole world, and in your city, many of our Christian men exorcising them

in the Name of Jesus Christ . . . have healed and do heal, rendering helpless and/or driving the possessing devils out of the men, though they could not be cured by all the other exorcists, and those who used incantations and drugs.[3]

The Montanists

The first recorded schism in Church history occurred as a result of a revival of the *pneumatika*.[4] Montanus, of Phrygia in Asia Minor, had a Pentecostal experience at his baptism: He spoke in tongues and began prophesying, declaring that the Paraclete, the Holy Spirit promised in the Gospel of John, was using him as his mouthpiece.[5] This man's experience in the Spirit set aflame a revival of great influence in the Church. Called the New Prophecy by its supporters, the Phrygian Heresy ("the heresy of slaves," to paraphrase) by its opponents, and Montanism by later theologians, this movement was characterized by fasting, asceticism, visions, voices, and the possession of the Spirit.

The renewal quickly spread to Rome, particularly among the Phrygian population. It even had its own worship center on the Palatine Hill, side-by-side with the pagan sanctuary of the Great Mother, who was also worshiped in spiritual ecstasy and frenzy. Initially, because Rome had always had her prophets and inspired men, the more traditional form of Roman Christianity was in harmony with moderate Montanism.

Enter Praxeas. According to Tertullian, Praxeas "crucified the Father and drove away the Paraclete." That is, he introduced the Monarchian gospel that the almighty Father died on Calvary, and he put to flight the holy dove of the New Prophecy by encouraging the official rejection of the Phrygians belief and experience. Originally, the Roman bishop had recognized the New Prophecy when Praxeas first arrived in Rome, but Praxeas soon convinced him to withdraw his "letters of peace." "This," Carrington writes, "is an important moment in Roman church history."[6] For the first time on record, the Church was faced with "official" division.

Irenaeus, who himself was not a Montanist, nevertheless was sympathetic with a more moderate form of prophetism. Irenaeus proudly claims:

> ... Those who are in truth His disciples, receiving grace from Him, do in His name perform [miracles], so as to promote the welfare of other men, according to the gift which each one has received from Him. For some do certainly and truly drive out devils, so that those who have thus been cleansed from evil spirits frequently both believe [in Christ] and join themselves to the Church. Others have foreknowledge of things to come: they see visions, and utter prophetic expressions. Others still heal the sick by laying their hands upon them, and they are made whole. Yea, moreover, as I have said, the dead even have been raised up, and remained among us for many years. And what shall I more say? It is not possible to name the number of the gifts which the Church [scattered] throughout the whole world, has received from God, in the Name of Jesus Christ . . . and which she exerts day by day for the benefit of the Gentiles. . . . For as she has received freely from God, freely also does she minister [to others] . . . She has been accustomed to work miracles for the advantage of mankind, and not lead them into error.[7]

The editors of the *Ante-Nicene Fathers* add an interesting footnote to Irenaeus' declaration:

> The reader will not fail to remark this highly interesting testimony, that the divine charismata bestowed upon the infant church were not wholly extinct in the days of Irenaeus.[8]

Rebuking those who opposed Phrygianism, Irenaeus wrote:

> In their desire to frustrate the gifts of the Spirit which have been poured out according to the pleasure of the Father upon the human race in these times, they do not accept that aspect [of the evangelical dispensation] presented by John's Gospel, in which the Lord promised that He would send the Paraclete; but set aside at once both the Gospel and the prophetic Spirit. Wretched men indeed! Who wish to be pseudo-prophets, forsooth, but who set aside the gifts of prophecy from the church. . . . For, in his Epistle to the Corinthians, he speaks expressly of prophetical gifts, and recognized men and women prophesying in the Church. Sinning, therefore, in all these particulars, against the Spirit of God, they fall into the irremissible sin.[9]

Irenaeus' argument in this excerpt is especially applicable to the current debate over the contemporary exercise of the *pneumatika*. First, he argues by implication that the coming of the Spirit prophesied in John 14 and 15 is not merely the promise of a highly personal, individualized, and silent experience deep in the individual's heart. Rather, Irenaeus suggests that there is something visible about the coming of the Spirit, something powerful, something evident. This is certainly borne out by the book of Acts.

Second, Irenaeus argues from 1 Corinthians that the experience of the Spirit, particularly in prophecy, is to be a fundamental element of church life. First Corinthians is recognized as authoritative, and what Paul has written is accepted at face value. He makes no attempt to "explain it away."

Third, Irenaeus makes a connection between the rejection of the supernatural ministry of the Holy Spirit and the unpardonable sin (Matthew 12:31), which parallels precisely the teaching of Jesus on this subject. He, too, like the Phrygians, was accused of ministering miracles by another Spirit. We hear a familiar ring in the popular objection to the *pneumatika:* "Speaking in tongues is of the devil."

Irenaeus writes of other examples of the supernatural:

> And so far are they from being able to raise the dead [referring to the false teachers], as the Lord raised them, and the apostles did by means of prayer, and as has been frequently done in the brotherhood on account of some necessity—the entire church in that particular locality entreating with much fasting and prayer, the spirit of the dead man had returned.[10]
>
> ... We do also hear many brethren in the church, who through the Spirit speak all kinds of languages [Eusebius substitutes the word "tongues" in his quotation of this passage; see Eusebius, History, v. 7.61], and bring to light for the general benefit the hidden things of men, and declare the mysteries of God, whom also the apostle terms "spiritual," they being spiritual because they partake of the Spirit.[11]

Tertullian

The Montanists found their greatest champion in Tertullian, who converted to the sect in the middle of his life, sometime around the beginning of the third century. Tertullian wrote of miracles, healing, and, of course, prophetic utterance which was so prominent in the teaching of the Montanists.

Tertullian on healing:

> Even Severus himself, the father of Antonine [the emperor], was graciously mindful of the Christians, for he sought out the Christian Proculus, surnamed Torpacion, the steward of Euthodias, and in gratitude for his having once cured him

by anointing he kept him in his palace till the day of his death....[12]

Tertullian on dreams:

But from God—who has promised, indeed, "to pour out the grace of the Holy Spirit upon all flesh, and has ordained that His servants and His handmaids should see visions as well as utter prophecies"—must all those visions be regarded as emanating, which may be compared to the actual grace of God, as being honest, holy, prophetic, inspired, instructive, inviting to virtue.[13]

This reference to dreams and visions as a consequence of the outpouring of the Holy Spirit is part of Tertullian's apology for the "ecstasy" of the Montanists. His point is that mere ecstasy is not intrinsically evil. What is at issue here is the cause of the ecstasy. If the cause is the Holy Spirit, then whatever issues from this kind of ecstasy is "honest, holy, prophetic, inspired, instructive, inviting to virtue."

Tertullian on miracle-working prayer:

Marcus Aurelius also, in his expedition to Germany, by the prayers his Christian soldiers offered to God, got rain in that well known thirst. When, indeed, have not droughts been put away by our kneelings and our fastings?[14]

Tertullian, writing about ecstatic prophecy, challenges Marcion to produce anything like the true gifts of the Spirit:

Let Marcion then exhibit, as gifts of his god, some prophets, such as have not spoken by human sense, but with the Spirit of God, such as have both predicted things to come, and have made manifest the secrets of the hearts—only let it be by the Spirit, in an ecstasy, that is, in rapture, whenever an interpretation of tongues has occurred to him.[15]

In this same chapter, Tertullian also makes a direct connection between the gifts of the Spirit enumerated in 1 Corinthians 12 and the promise of the outpouring of the Spirit fulfilled on the day of Pentecost.

> Now was absolutely fulfilled that promise of the Spirit which was given by the word of Joel.... Since, then, the Creator promised the gift of His Spirit in the latter days; and since Christ has in these last days appeared as the dispenser of spiritual gifts ... it evidently follows in connection with this prediction of the last days, that this gift of the Spirit belongs to Him who is the Christ of the predicters. Now compare the Spirit's specific graces, as they are described by the apostle ... "to one is given...."[16]

Contemporary Application of the Montanist Controversy

The Montanist schism contains some valuable lessons for the current debate over the *pneumatika*. There were, indeed, problems with the movement that have close parallels with the present renewal of the Spirit. First, people always seem to go overboard with ecstatic prophecy. Then, as now, there was a real need for judgment and accountability as Paul describes in 1 Corinthians 4:1–2. Carrington writes: "... Full recognition was being extended to the prophets, their gifts, and their oracles, which probably meant the reception of their scriptures for reading in the church."[17] Whenever people feel they have the capacity for special revelation, there exists the potential for that revelation to be elevated to a level equal to or even surpassing Scripture.

In the case of the Montanists, their position finally became so extreme that total prophetic authority was concentrated in one place—Montanus' hometown in Phrygia. "The voice of God himself was being heard in the valleys of Phrygia; and this new fact constituted it the center of the universal church, a doctrine which soon assumed authoritative form."[18] This gave rise to questions about the authority of the Church and the completeness of biblical revelation. The canonical books of the Bible must remain our standard of faith, practice, and authority, or we will have no standard.

Secondly, it had been agreed by both orthodox church leaders and the Montanists alike that "prophecy was a gift which should continue in the whole church to the end of time.[19] The problem, however, was whether or not prophecy should be delivered in ecstasy. The apostle Paul gives guidance on this issue: "And the spirits of the prophets are subject to the prophets" (1 Corinthians 14:32), which suggests that the prophetic urge is not uncontrollable.

Finally, "in doctrine, Montanism was no heresy."[20] Tertullian himself asserted his identity with the orthodox beliefs of the Church in his famous "Rule of Faith."[21] Similarly, the present-day renewal of the Holy Spirit is generally evangelical and orthodox.

Selections from Origen

After arguing for the importance of the testimony of miracles in the ministry of Jesus and the apostles, Origen writes of the post-apostolic age:

> And there is still preserved among Christians traces of that Holy Spirit which appeared in the form of a dove. They expel evil spirits, and perform many cures, and foresee certain events, according to the will of the Logos. And . . . many have been converted to Christianity as if against their will some sort of spirit having suddenly transformed their minds . . . having appeared to them either in a waking vision or dream of the night.[22]

Earlier in his same defense against Celsus, Origen wrote:

> ... The Gospel has a demonstration of its own, more divine
> than any established by Grecian dialectics. And this divine
> method is called by the apostle the "manifestation of the
> Spirit and of power" ... "power" because of the signs and
> wonders which we must believe to have been performed ...
> and ... that traces of them are still preserved among those
> who regulate their lives by the precepts of the Gospel.[23]

Near the end of his defense, Origen writes with great conviction,

> And the name of Jesus can still remove distractions from
> the minds of men, and expel demons, and also take away diseases; and produce a marvellous meekness of spirit and complete change of character.[24]

Cyprian, in one of his numerous epistles, wrote of baptism
as an instrument of physical and spiritual healing:

> ... Those who are baptized by urgent necessity in sickness,
> and obtain grace, are free from the unclean spirit wherewith
> they were previously moved, and live in the church in praise
> and honor, and day by day make more and more advances in
> the increase of heavenly grace by the growth of their faith.[25]

The Desert Fathers

Sometime during the second century, a number of monks
began leaving the Nile Valley to retreat to the more austere
setting of the surrounding deserts. As this movement of isolation and incredible self-discipline spread into Palestine and
the deserts of Syria and Asia Minor, these zealots become
known informally as the "Desert Fathers." Theirs was a life

of self-abasement and extended meditation, fasting and prayer. It is not surprising that accounts of miracles and other unusual phenomena have come to us from this mystical environment. The following examples have been gleaned from *The Sayings of the Desert Fathers*, translated by Benedicta Ward.

Abba ("Father") David relates the story of the healing and deliverance of the daughter of an important person. When the monk reached the house, the possessed woman slapped him. But he only turned the other cheek. The devil, tortured by this, cried out, "What violence! The commandment of Jesus drives me out." Immediately the woman was cleansed.[26]

Abba Longinus, who had not disclosed his identity, was shown by a woman where she was suffering. He made the sign of the cross over the sore and sent her away saying, "Go, and God will heal you, for Longinus cannot help you at all." The monk had refused to identify himself, deliberately avoiding the woman's adoration. She had no notion that it was the great Father to whom she was speaking, yet the woman went away confident, and she was healed on the spot.[27]

In another recorded incident, Poimen said of Histeros that he was like the serpent of brass that Moses made for the healing of the people; he possessed all virtue, and without speaking, he healed everyone.[28]

This same Poimen had a member of his family whose child's face was turned backwards. Poimen "... groaning, stood up and prayed, 'God, heal your creature, that he be not ruled by the enemy.' " When he had made the sign of the cross, the child was healed immediately and given back whole to his father.[29]

Perhaps one could make a connection between mysticism and miracles. Manifestations of the supernatural seemed to be most in evidence among the mystics and the deeply spiritual of the early Church, principally the Montanists and the early monastics. Latourette writes of the famed monk Anthony: ". . . Many sought him out, some for spiritual counsel and others for the miraculous healing of their disease."[30] Could it be that an intellectualization of the revelation of Scripture leads to a paucity of divine "signs"?

In 1 Corinthians 2, Paul addresses this issue by making a distinction between the thinking of the natural man and the mind of the spiritual (*pneumatikos*). Earlier in this chapter, the apostle affirms, "And my speech and my preaching was not with enticing words of man's wisdom, but in demonstration of the Spirit and of power" (verse 4).

The *Pneumatika* in the Third and Fourth Centuries

By the end of the third century Eusebius was writing his *History*. Although he speaks with favor about the miracles of former centuries, his report has a hollow ring, perhaps because reports of miracles were becoming infrequent. Before quoting Irenaeus on the subject of the miraculous, he comments, "In the second book of the same treatise he [Irenaeus] shows that manifestations of divine and miraculous power continued to his time in some of the churches."[31]

There are other reports in later literature, but the accounts begin to take on more of an apocryphal flavor. Socrates records several such miracles in his *Ecclesiastical History*. He mentions the "extraordinary miracles" performed by Paphnutius, a bishop of one of the cities of upper Thebes (I.11), the unusual miracles of Eutychian the Monk (I.13), as well as the desert monks of Egypt: "On reaching these solitudes they found the monks engaged in their customary exercises, praying, healing diseases, and casting out devils. Yet they [their persecutors], regardless of these extraordinary evidences of Divine power, suffered them not to continue their solemn devotions" (IV.24).

Socrates also records the unusual disappearance of baptismal water when the church tried to baptize a certain imposter. "As [he] was taken there [to the baptismal font], the water vanished as before" (VII.17). And in Book VII, Chapter 39, Socrates reports the miraculous preservation of a church building, in response to fervent prayer, during a great conflagration in the city of Constantinople.

Augustine

In the writings of the great Augustine we detect a different theological perspective on miracles and the *pneumatika*, a view that undoubtedly has had a great impact on the Christian view of the miraculous through the centuries. For the first time one can ascertain a subtle admission that the age of miracles had ceased, and that now God was speaking to his Church through other means. A telling statistic can be found by a quick review of the Scripture indexes to the writings of Augustine in the several volumes of his work collected in *The Nicene and Post Nicene Fathers*. In the thousands of pages of Augustine's massive works, there are fewer than a dozen references to 1 Corinthians 14 (the exercise of the charismata), while in bold contrast there are approximately 200 references to 1 Corinthians 15 (the resurrection chapters)! Almost as numerous are his citings of 1 Corinthians 13 (charity chapter), and Augustine frequently alludes to "charity" being more desirable than the power of working miracles (*Commentary on Psalm 130*).

On the Profit of Believing, 30, Augustine writes,

> In another place, where I had made mention of the miracles, which our Lord Jesus did, while He was here in the flesh, I added, saying, "Why say you, do not those things take place now?" And I answered, "Because they would not move unless they were wonderful, and if they were usual they would not be wonderful."

In another work, *Sermons On New Testament Lessons, Sermon XXXVII,* his argument is even clearer:

> These things then the Lord did [miracles] to invite us to the faith. This faith reigneth now in the church, which is spread throughout the whole world, and now He worketh greater cures on account of which He disdained not then to exhibit those lesser ones. For as the soul is better than the body, so is the saving health of the soul better than the health of the body.

Augustine's view here is influenced not only by the waning of miracle-working power in the Church, but also, I suspect, by the influence of the Platonic world view that gives much closer attention to soul, or immaterial aspects of man, than to the body. (I take issue with this idea, by the way, because it is not in harmony with the incarnation. "We are bought with a price," Paul proclaims, "therefore, glorify God in your *bodies.*" The most sacred, continuing ordinance of the Church, the Lord's Table, cannot be celebrated without eating and drinking; profoundly, the celebration of the Eucharist depends on our bodies. Even as we are bound to the Lord by the Spirit, so also Jesus is bound to us in his humanity. God is concerned about the whole being of man—spirit, soul, and body (1 Thessalonians 5:23).)

The Reformation and Later Centuries

Calvin, in referring to tongues, wrote:

> At present great theologians ... declaim against them with furious zeal. As it is certain that the Holy Spirit has here honored the use of tongues with never-dying praise, we may very readily gather, what is the kind of spirit that actuates these reformers, who level as many reproaches as they can against the pursuit of them. ... Paul, nevertheless, commends the use of tongues. So far is he from wishing them abolished or thrown away.[32]

John Wesley, in a letter to a friend, the Reverend Dr. Middleton, wrote:

> I must observe a historical mistake which occurs toward the bottom of your next page. Since the Reformation, you say: "This gift [tongues] has never once been heard of, or pretended to, by the Romanists themselves." But has it been pretended to (whether justly or not) by no others, though not by the Romanists? Has it never once been heard of since that time? Sir, your memory failed you again. ... It has been heard of more than once, no farther off than the valleys of the Dauphiny [France].[33]

Thomas Walsh, one of Wesley's foremost preachers, wrote in his diary this record dated March 18, 1750:

> This morning the Lord gave me a language that I knew not of, raising my soul to Him in a wonderful manner.[34]

R. Boyd, an intimate friend of D. L. Moody, wrote in his *Trials and Triumphs of Faith* (1874),

When I, a Y.M.C.A. member, got to the rooms of the Young Men's Christian Association, I found the meeting "on fire." The young men were speaking with tongues, prophesying. What on earth did it mean? Only that Moody had been addressing them that afternoon. What manner of man is this, thought I, but I still did not give him my hand . . . Many of the clergy were so opposed to the movement that they turned their backs upon our poor, innocent Young Men's Christian Association, for the part we took in the work; but afterward, when the floodgates of Divine grace were opened, Sunderland was taken by storm. I cannot describe Moody's great meeting; I can only say that the people of Sunderland warmly supported the movement, in spite of their local advisors.[35]

Charles Finney wrote in his autobiography, *Memoirs of Rev. Charles E. Finney, Written by Himself* (1875),

I returned to the front office, and found that the fire that I had made of large wood was nearly burned out. But as I turned and was about to take a seat by the fire, I received a mighty baptism of the Holy Ghost. Without any expectation of it, without any recollection that I had ever heard the thing mentioned by any person in the world, the Holy Spirit descended upon me in a manner that seemed to go through me, body and soul. I could feel the impression like a wave of electricity, going through me. Indeed, it seemed to come in waves and waves of liquid love; for I could not express it in any other way. It seemed like the very breath of God. I can recollect distinctly that it seemed to fan me, like immense wings.

Nineteenth-century instances of tongues-speaking may be traced to a revival in Port Glasgow, Scotland, led by James and George MacDonald, men of unimpeachable character. In 1830 Dr. Thompson, a lay member of Regent's Square Presbyterian Church in London, carried news of this revival to his pastor, Edward Irving. People in Irving's church

sought and received a Pentecostal experience of the baptism
in the Spirit, and began to speak in tongues and prophesy in
public services. The revival spread to Sweden, Ireland, and
Armenia. The London congregation was soon divided by controversy and forced to form a new denomination, the Catholic Apostolic Church. Self-appointed "apostles and prophets"
soon usurped Irving's authority and interrupted his preaching and Communion.[36]

In 1901, a number of students at the Bethel Bible College
in Topeka, Kansas, experienced a Pentecostal outpouring
under the leadership of Charles Fox Parham. This fire spread
to California, where in 1906 another great stirring of the
Spirit occurred at the famed Azusa Street Mission in Los Angeles. It was these revivals early in this century that gave
birth to modern Pentecostalism. (For a thorough history of
modern Pentecostalism see: *The Pentecostals,* by John
Thomas Nichol[37] and *With Signs Following,* by Stanley Frodsham.[38])

For the next sixty years the Pentecostal experience remained a distinctive and "peculiar" practice of the traditional Pentecostal of "full gospel" denominations—
Assemblies of God, Foursquare, and Pentecostal Church of
God, to name a few. During the 1950s the world became familiar with great healing ministries, like those of Oral Roberts, T. L. Osborn, and Kathryn Kuhlman; and in the last
decade speaking in tongues has been witnessed with increas-
ing frequency among traditional churches.

Today Pentecostalism is no longer a cryptic, isolated phenomenon. Neo-Pentecostalism (the New Pentecost, the charismatic renewal) has had an impact on every major
denomination in America and has influenced millions of lives.

Chapter Fourteen

The Abiding Apostolic Ministry

THE TESTIMONY OF SCRIPTURE is that signs and wonders will follow those who believe, and Church history confirms that the Holy Spirit has continued to speak with special power from those first days when the chosen twelve ministered with signs and wonders. Yet these twelve had a special office, that of apostle, and one that we don't hear much about today. Are there no present-day apostles? Was that a special office reserved for the twelve?

First, let's remember that miracles and signs will follow "them that believe," not just apostles (Mark 16:17). A case in point is Philip the evangelist. We read of his ministry in Acts 8:6–7: "And the people with one accord gave heed unto those things which Philip spake, hearing and seeing the miracles which he did. For unclean spirits, crying with loud voice, came out of many that were possessed with them: and many taken with palsies, and that were lame, were healed." Philip was not called an apostle; he was one of the brethren of the Church (Acts 6:5) and an evangelist.

Another example is Ananias, "a certain disciple at Damascus" (Acts 9:10). We are not told that he had any official position in the church, yet the Lord spoke to him in a vision (Acts 9:10) and performed a miracle of healing in answer to his prayers (Acts 9:17–18).

Actually, the idea that the sign gifts have died out often stems from the feeling that they were the exclusive prerogative of the twelve, and when the twelve died, the gifts ceased. The New Testament narrative, however, gives no indication that this special office would cease functioning with the death of the twelve. In fact, there is much evidence that apostolic ministry continued through the close of the canon. For example, Barnabus, not among the twelve, is called an apostle in Acts 14:14.

Another New Testament reference to the continuing ministry of apostleship is found in Paul's defense of the resurrection in 1 Corinthians 15. In verse 5 of this chapter Paul testifies that Jesus, after his death, "was seen . . . of the twelve [apostles]." But in verse 7 he adds: "After that, he was seen of James; *then of all the apostles*." Gordon Clark writes, "This phrase includes the twelve, but it includes others also. The wording indicates that James is included . . . [and] the word [all the apostles] is more inclusive than 'The Twelve.'"[1]

In 2 Corinthians 8:23 Paul seems to recognize Titus as one of the apostles (*apostoloi*), incorrectly rendered "messengers" in the King James. The same misleading KJV translation is found in Philippians 2:25 where Epaphroditus is called "your messenger." Again, this is the Greek term *apostolos*. Another reference to apostles other than The Twelve is recorded in 1 Thessalonians 2:6 where the phrase "we . . . apostles" includes Paul, Timothy, and Silas (see 1 Thessalonians 1:1; 2 Thessalonians 1:1; Acts 17:11–15).

Apostleship as an abiding ministry is also confirmed by Revelation 2:2, which speaks of false apostles. If true apostolic ministry had been confined to the twelve alone, why would the Lord Himself commend the church at Ephesus, founded by no less an apostle than Paul, for trying "them which say they are apostles, and are not"? For every counterfeit dollar there must be genuine currency. Without the continuation of genuine apostolic ministry there would have been no need for our Lord's commendation. Revelation, the book from which we derive this key reference, was written near the end of the first century. Eleven of the original twelve apostles had already "died out," but there remained a continuing need to try "them which say they are apostles." If the early Church, like some theologians today, had limited apostolic ministry to the original twelve, the hoax of "them which say there are apostles" would have been ignored.

It is also argued that Paul and the other early apostles performed miracles because they did not have what the Church has today—the completed canon of Scripture. This objection ignores an important feature of the book of Acts and the New Testament epistles: The preaching of the early apostles was firmly grounded in the Scriptures (see Acts 3:24; 17:11; 26:22). They had the Word! They even had the testimony of Jesus, later recorded by Luke in his Gospel: "If they hear not Moses and the prophets, neither will they be persuaded, though one rose from the dead" (Luke 16:31).

Miracles will never save the soul; only a heart commitment to God's Word can do that (1 Peter 1:22–23). This is a truth the early apostles understood fully, yet they still believed in the importance of miracles.

In 1 Corinthians 12:28 Paul gives apostleship preeminence as a ministry in the Body of Christ: "And God hath set some in the church, first apostles, secondarily prophets, thirdly teachers, after that miracles. . . ." This is also the teaching of Ephesians 4:11–13 where "apostle" is again listed first among the gift ministries. These verses in Ephesians 4 represent the most powerful New Testament statement in support of continuing apostolic ministry. The ministries given in verse 11, apostles, prophets, evangelists, pastors, and teachers, have a threefold purpose: "For the perfecting of the saints, for the work of the ministry, for the edifying of the body of Christ" (verse 12). The verse that follows tells us that these ministries, apostleship included, are to perfect, work, and edify, "Till we all come in the unity of the faith, and of the knowledge of the Son of God, unto a perfect man, unto the measure of the stature of the fulness of Christ."

Obviously, this glorious consummation is yet to be realized, which means we can safely conclude that the ministry of apostleship is still necessary in the Church today. Apostolic ministry in the New Testament is characterized by the ability to establish churches, miracle-working power, and doctrinal authority. If the perfecting of the Body depends even in part on the office of the apostle, we must never banish this important ministry from the Church.

Chapter Fifteen

Preaching and Prophecy

THERE HAS BEEN much debate on the nature of prophecy and the office of the prophet. This ministry, in the full New Testament sense, is simply not operative in non-charismatic churches. Hence, those who oppose charismatic practice generally hold one of two views.

First, if the teaching of the New Testament on prophecy is taken at face value, then the absence of such a unique ministry forces the conclusion that the gift was temporary and ceased with the gift of apostleship. The classic expositor, Albert Barnes, after defining prophecy as a unique revelation gift, concludes: "The office or the endowment was temporary, designed for the settlement and establishment of the Church; and then, like the apostolic office, having accomplished its purpose, was to cease."[1]

Vine proposes a similar, though not as strong, view: "With

117

the completion of the canon of Scripture prophecy apparently passed away."[2] "Apparently" implies that he believes the gift disappeared, but cannot explain why because the Scriptures are not clear on the subject. Vine can only cite 1 Corinthians 13:8–9, a passage I discussed in Chapter 5.

Additionally, I have already evaluated this interpretation offered by Barnes, Vine, and others, in the preceding chapter. To reiterate, if apostleship is a vital organ in the Body of Christ and is necessary for the perfecting of the saints, so is prophecy. If any one of the ministries mentioned in Ephesians 4:11–13 is valid and necessary, all are valid and necessary. Prophecy is a gift and office revealed as an integral feature of the New Testament Church.

Second, the view opposing the continuation of prophecy holds that it is merely another word for preaching. As a consequence, prophecy loses its identity as a unique gift. In other words, the prophet is the preacher and the one who preaches is manifesting the gift of prophecy. An example of this is found in the *Living Bible* paraphrase of 1 Corinthians 12–14. Repeatedly, when the word *prophetes*, "prophet," occurs in the original Greek, it is translated "one who preaches the messages of God." A case in point is 14:3: "But one who prophesies, preaching the messages of God, is helping others grow in the Lord, encouraging and comforting them."[3] Beck paraphrases this verse, "But when you speak God's Word, you talk to people to help them grow."[4] Beck omits the word "prophet" entirely. A careful study of the New Testament, however, demonstrates that the terms rendered "prophet" and "preacher" are *not* synonymous.

Here is Barnes' definition of prophecy in full:

The prophets were distinguished from the teachers *(didiskaloi)*, "in that while the latter spoke in a calm, connected, didactic discourse adapted to instruct the hearers, the prophet spoke more from the impulse of sudden inspiration, from the light of a sudden revelation at the moment (I Cor. xiv, 30, *apokalyphthe*), and his discourse was probably more adapted, by means of powerful exhortation, to awaken the feelings and conscience of the hearers." The idea of speaking from revelation, he [Robinson] adds, seems to be fundamental to the correct idea of the nature of the prophecy here referred to . . . the gift of prophetic instruction . . . [occurred] under the immediate influences of the Holy Spirit.[5]

In Kittel we read of the use of *prophetes* in relation to the ancient Greek oracle, the place where the gods were consulted for specific revelation and direction. This term

. . . denotes appointed men and women and their work, which is to declare something whose content is not derived from themselves but from the god who reveals his will at the particular site. This revelation is through direct inspiration or through signs which stand in need of human interpretation.[6]

There can be no doubt that *prophetes* belongs to the religious sphere, where it denotes the one who speaks in the name of a god, declaring the divine will and counsel in the oracle. Historical seers and prophets not connected with an oracle are never called *prophetai* but *chresmologoi* or the like.[7]

In reference to the New Testament prophet, the sixth volume of Kittel's *Dictionary* states:

The primitive Christian prophet is a man of full self-awareness. When he is speaking he can break off if a revelation is given to someone else. When two or more prophets have spoken in the congregation others may remain silent even though something is revealed to them. I Cor. 14:29. They cannot influence the revelation itself. *This comes from God with no co-operation on their part.* But the proclamation of what is revealed to them is according to their own will and it does not have to follow at once . . . The responsible person-hood of the prophet remains intact *even though the whole man with his understanding and will remains under the oper-ation of the Spirit. . . . Prophecy and speaking in tongues have much in common* since both are in a special way the work of the Spirit. They are obviously related in Acts 19:6.[8]

Trench's comments on the ministry of New Testament prophecy are also significant:

It is not discord and disorder but a higher harmony and a diviner order, which are introduced into his [the prophet's] soul; so that he is not as one overborne in the region of his lower life by forces stronger than his own, by an insurrection from beneath: but his spirit is lifted out of that region into a clearer atmosphere, a diviner day. . . . All that he had before still remains his, only purged, exalted, quickened by a power higher than his own; for man is most truly man when he is filled with the fulness of God.[9]

Thus, prophecy is a direct manifestation of the Spirit (1 Corinthians 12:7), not just preaching or polished oratory. "Manifestation" is a translation of the Greek work *phan-erosis*, which means a "bringing to light, a disclosure." The nine gifts of the Spirit labeled "manifestations" in 1 Corinth-ians 12, prophecy included, are means by which the Holy Spirit manifests Himself through members of the Body of Christ. These charismatic gifts are open disclosures of the Spirit. Although the Spirit makes Himself known in men's hearts through the inner voice, these nine gifts in 1 Corinth-ians 12 are special and direct manifestations of the person and power of the Holy Spirit.

If prophesying, *propheteuo*, is a direct manifestation of the Holy Spirit, what is preaching, *kerusso*? The etymologies of these two terms differ as much as their respective uses in the New Testament.

Kerusso is most frequently found in ancient literature outside the New Testament in the noun form *kerux*, which means "herald."

> An external attribute is required of a herald. He has to have a good voice. Apart from the predominant question of voice, certain qualities of character were required. . . . It is demanded that they deliver their message as it is given to them. The *essential point* [not exact words, as in the case of the prophet] about the report which they give is that it does not originate with them. Behind it stands a higher power. The herald does not express his own views. He is the spokesman for his master. . . . Heralds adopt the mind of those who commission them. . . . The stoic philosopher is a divine herald of this kind. . . . The stoic had a profound sense of having a special God-given task among men. The deity revealed his secret to him, and he must now bear witness to it. Through him God Himself speaks, his teaching is revelation, his preaching the Word of God. To despise his word and refuse to follow his teaching is to do despite to God. . . . The relationship between these preachers and the early Christian missionaries has often been noted. Both are divine messengers. Both have a higher mission. Both bring to men a new message which offers salvation. There is little distinction as regards the mode of their activity. Their work consists of *kerussein*, in the loud publication of the message entrusted to them [italics mine].[10]

Oddly enough, though the term so well describes the work of the Christian preacher, *kerux* is found only three times in the New Testament (1 Timothy 2:7; 2 Timothy 1:11; 2 Peter 2:5).

> How are we to explain the reserve with which the Bible views the term? In many respects *kerux* seems to be a very

suitable term to describe the Christian preacher. It has many links with *apostolos* and is also at many points an equivalent of *euaggelos* [evangelist]. Nevertheless, the NT manifestly avoids it. Why? ... The Bible is not telling us about human preachers; it is telling us about the preaching ... Hence *kerussein* [preaching] is more important than the *kerux* [preacher] in the NT.[11]

In the New Testament,

> ... *kerussein* does not mean the delivery of a learned and edifying or hortatory discourse in well-chosen words and a pleasant voice. It is the declaration of an event. Its true sense is "to proclaim." ... Preaching is not a lecture on the nature of God's kingdom. It is a proclamation, the declaration of an event. If Jesus came to preach, this means that He was sent to announce the *basileia tou theou* [kingdom of God] and therewith bring it.[12]

Thus, the one who preaches proclaims the essence of the gospel message, while the one who prophesies proclaims the very words of the Holy Spirit. The terms *prophet* and *herald* are not synonymous, and "prophesying" and "preaching" are not identical activities. There may be certain similarities, but the actions are as different from one another as the use of these terms in the original language.

Prophecy is not inspired preaching. To confuse the terms is to deny the operation of the special New Testament gift of prophecy. "A preacher usually prepares, speaks, and expounds from the Word of God," writes Michael Harper. "But a prophet speaks directly under the anointing of the Holy Spirit. Both have a part to play in the edification of the church—but they should not be confused."[13]

Chapter Sixteen

Charismatic Worship: Reverent or Riotous?

WHILE THE REAL ISSUE is whether or not charismatic worship and praise is biblical, opposition often focuses on these objections: It's emotionalism. It's irreverent. It's confusion. Are these accusations legitimate? Is charismatic worship enthusiastic to the point of being distasteful?

Stendahl says there is room in religion for "ecstasy":

Glossolalia is a facet of what I like to see as high-voltage religion. It is obvious to me that to some people, and in some situations, the experience of God is so overwhelming that charismatic phenomena are the "natural" expression. In the history of religions and of the church there is an honorable place for ecstasy. Who said that only rational words or silence

123

would be proper. As a preacher and lecturer, I even wonder if it is not wise to let glossolalia gush forth in the church so that those who are not professional in the shaping of words are free to express fully their overwhelmed praise to the Lord. Actually, in the history of the church the practice of glossolalia has often had a democratizing effect . . . through which in a certain sense, "the last have become first."[1]

Some time ago our church was renting a very large, old structure for its services. Above each main entrance into the auditorium were posted the solemn words SILENCE. ENTERING THE HOUSE OF GOD. It was not long before someone covered the word SILENCE with a handwritten inscription, REJOICE, making the caption read, REJOICE! ENTERING THE HOUSE OF GOD. Paul the apostle was no less enthusiastic when he wrote, "Rejoice in the Lord always: and again I say, Rejoice" (Philippians 4:4). There is a place for silence, but there is also a place for joy unspeakable and full of glory.

Is charismatic worship irreverent? Some have complained that charismatics do not have to shout at God; He is not deaf. But God dwells in the praises of His people, and the Bible frequently records incidents of high-volume, high-intensity praise. According to the book of Revelation, God graciously and gloriously receives praise and adoration so thunderous that it is described as having the sound of many waters. And when Jesus drew near Jerusalem just prior to His week of Passion, "the whole multitude of the disciples began to rejoice and praise God with a loud voice for all the mighty works that they had seen" (Luke 19:37). Do we have any less reason to shout His praise today? As Charles Wesley wrote, "Oh, for a thousand tongues to sing my great Redeemer's praise!" If the disciples of the Lord hold their peace, "the stones would immediately cry out" (Luke 19:40). This verse suggests that on certain occasions, *silence* is irreverent!

Particularly offensive to non-Pentecostals, I understand, is when "the whole church speaks in tongues." The verses commonly referred to here are 1 Corinthians 14:27–28: "If any man speak in an unknown tongue . . . let one interpret. But if there be no interpreter, let him keep silence in the church." This seems to indicate that corporate speaking in tongues is wrong. But is this really what these verses are teaching? True, speaking in tongues can be out-of-order, offensive, and confusing. But Paul's appeal for silence in the church is not as absolute as some would lead us to believe. Why?

First, the context of 1 Corinthians 14 is not ministering to the Lord in corporate worship, but ministering to the Body. The edification of the church is the key issue, reflected by such statements as "That the church may receive edifying" (verse 5), and "In the church I had rather speak five words with my understanding, that by my voice I might teach others also" (verse 19). It is in this specific regard that Paul directs the church in the matter of tongues spoken "by two, or at the most by three," and the need for interpretation. In contrast, when the Spirit was poured out on the day of Pentecost and later upon the house of Cornelius, everyone was speaking in tongues at once about the wonderful works of God, and there is no mention of interpretation for those who did not understand the message. The context of these chapters is worship, not Body ministry (see Acts 2:4; 10:46).

Second, the Greek term rendered "silence" is a word that can be translated "to hold one's peace."[2] It does not always denote absolute silence. For example, this term is used in 1 Corinthians 14:35 where women are told to keep silent—silent in terms of self-assertiveness and impropriety, not praise and worship. They are to hold their peace.

Third, the second half of verse 28 in 1 Corinthians 14 is the decisive point that often goes unnoticed: "But if there be no interpreter, let him keep silence in the church; *and let him speak to himself, and to God.*" Let him speak! Since in this context the speaking refers to tongues, how is it possible for a person to speak in tongues to himself and to God *without speaking?* Speaking in tongues is an audible verbalization of the languages of the Spirit. First Corinthians tells us plainly that the one speaking in an unknown tongue "*speaketh* not unto men, but unto God." If there is no one to interpret, at least let him speak quietly in tongues to God. Let him cease from self-assertive, ego-gratifying noise, but let him speak!

Actually, from a pragmatic point of view, if someone does speak aloud mistakenly in a tongue and no interpretation is forthcoming, no terrible harm is done. Doubtless no Christian, charismatic or not, believes that God demands absolute perfection in every moment of every worshp service. When we have done our very best we are still unprofitable servants. A Christian's mistake in the exercise of the gifts is not a calamity; it is simply another reminder of human imperfection and our need to put absolute trust in God alone.

The improper exercise of the spiritual gifts is only one area of biblical revelation where we fall short of God's perfect standards. Charismatics have made mistakes in using the gifts in the church, but most prefer erring in that direction over squelching the manifestations of the Spirit. Like the meteorologist who never influences the direction or velocity of the wind but merely reports its activity, so the charismatic hopes to give accurate expression to the movement of the Spirit (see John 3:8). "Quench not the Spirit. Despise not prophesyings" (1 Thessalonians 5:19–20) and "Forbid not to speak with tongues" (1 Corinthians 14:39).

Biblical Foundations

In addition to these Scripture references, there are other biblical foundation stones for charismatic worship and praise, relating in particular to the Book of Psalms. In Colossians 3:16 Paul tells us: "Let the word of Christ dwell in you richly in all wisdom; teaching and admonishing one another in *psalms* and hymns and spiritual songs, singing with grace in your hearts to the Lord." In Ephesians 5:18–19 we are commanded: ". . . Be filled with the Spirit; Speaking to yourselves in *psalms* and hymns and spiritual songs, singing and making melody in your heart to the Lord."

Twice in the context of Christian worship Paul suggests the instructive value of psalms. Frequently in the New Testament this Greek word, *psalmos,* is used specifically in reference to the Psalms of David (Luke 20:42, 24:44; Acts 1:20; 13:33). A. T. Robertson believes that the *psalmois* in Colossians 3:16 is a reference to "the Psalms in the Old Testament originally with musical accompaniment."[3] Barnes wrote in his commentary on Ephesians 5:19, "The psalms of David were sung by the Jews at the temple, and by the early Christians, and the singing of those psalms has constituted a delightful part of public worship in all ages."[4] A conservative branch of the Presbyterian church even contends that all three terms used in these verses ("psalms," "hymns," and "spiritual songs") refer directly to the Psalms of David.[5]

These verses in Colossians and Ephesians are speaking of the Old Testament Book of Psalms, which is to be a specific source of instruction and admonition for the Church—"teaching and admonishing one another with *psalms.*" The Psalms are not only lofty hymns of praise; they also tell us how to worship. For example, Psalm 47 enjoins: "Clap your hands, all ye people; shout unto God with the voice of triumph." And Psalm 149:2–3 directs us to "rejoice in him that made him: let the children of Zion be joyful in their King. Let them praise his name in the dance. . . ." If we are to teach and admonish one another with "psalms," we should be willing to affirm our obedience to the Word of the Lord by responding to its exhortations. "Be ye doers of the word, and not hearers only" (James 1:22).

The commandment in the Psalms to praise the Lord is no different from the command to lift up our hands in the sanctuary and bless the Lord. "Praise the Lord" tells us what to do; "lift up your hands" tells us how to do it. Is it right to obey the first of these commands while disregarding the second? The Psalms of David reveal at least six ways to praise the Lord: clapping, shouting, singing, dancing, playing musical instruments, and lifting hands. If one is valid, all must be valid. The Book of Psalms was the hymnbook of the early Church; it can be our hymnbook and order of worship today if we are willing to embrace its guidelines.

Acts 15:16 is another fascinating revelation of how the Psalms provide a pattern for worship. At the Jerusalem Council James spoke of the new covenant of grace and quoted the Old Testament prophet Amos (see Amos 9:11): "After this I will return, and will build again the tabernacle of David, which is fallen down." It is highly significant that James refers to the tabernacle of David, not the tabernacle of Moses. The tabernacle of David was unique in the Old Testament and presents a picture of the New Testament age of grace.

In the tabernacle of David the Ark of the Covenant, the dwelling place of Yahweh, was in full view. For a moment in history, between the days of the tabernacle of Moses and the age of Solomon's Temple, the veil was removed and the people beheld the manifested presence of the living God. It was before this unusual tabernacle on Mount Zion that David sang hymns of praise, wrote many of his psalms, and worshiped the God of his fathers without restraint. "Praise waiteth for thee, O God, *in Zion*" (Psalm 65:1).

In contrast, the Temple of Solomon was located on Mount Moriah. Only the tinkling of priestly bells and the screams of the sacrifices interrupted its stiff silence. But the tabernacle of David was erected with joy, singing, shouting, musical instruments, and dancing (1 Chronicles 15:25–29), and even after the dedication service certain of the Levites were appointed to offer special thanks to the God of Israel and to blow the trumpet continually before the Ark of the Covenant of God (1 Chronicles 16:4–6).[6]

Matthew Henry wrote, "This was but a tent, a poor, mean dwelling, yet this was the tabernacle, the temple, of which David, in his psalms, often speaks with so much affection. David, who pitched a tent for the ark, and continued steadfast to it, did far better than Solomon, who built a temple for it, and yet, in his latter end, turned his back upon it."[7]

Charismatics have not discovered the only acceptable form of worship. The living water of the Holy Spirit fits perfectly the contours of the vessel into which it is poured. Nevertheless, though it is criticized for its open displays of joy and praise, charismatic worship is grounded in the Word of God. Remember Michal, David's wife, who saw him joyfully transporting the ark of the covenant into Jerusalem? With religious contempt, she despised David in her heart because she saw him dancing in the streets (1 Chronicles 15:29). The sad consequence: She became unfruitful unto the day of her death (see 2 Samuel 6:14–16, 23). This is a sobering lesson for those who disdainfully reject charismatic effusiveness and joy.

The women of Israel danced for joy on the victory side of the Red Sea. David, with just a glimpse of grace, shouted enthusiastic praise before an Old Testament manifestation of the Lord's presence. The disciples of Jesus made "a joyful noise unto the Lord" when the King of glory entered Jerusalem *before* His vicarious death and victorious resurrection. Shall we, joint-heirs with Christ, seated with Him in heavenly places, worship the Lord with any less fervor than this great cloud of witnesses?

"After this I will return, and will build again *the tabernacle of David,* which is fallen down; and I will build again the ruins thereof, and I will set it up" (Acts 15:16).

Chapter Seventeen

Is Healing God's Will?

HEALING FOR THE BODY is an aspect of the atonement and is God's plan for His people. The finished work of Christ includes a restoration of everything that was lost in the Garden of Eden. According to the Genesis record, sin, sickness, pain, and the dominion of Satan are all consequences of the Fall, and Jesus came to reverse the curse.

"Christ hath redeemed us from the curse of the law" (Galatians 3:13), which includes sickness and disease (see Deuteronomy 28). Jesus was "made a curse for us: for it is written, Cursed is every one that hangeth on a tree" (Galatians 3:13). In the same context, Paul refers to Jesus as the "seed" of Abraham. Not coincidentally, Jesus is also the seed in the very first messianic prophecy in Genesis 3, where God promises an antidote for the curse and its consequences. The seed of the woman, it is foretold, would bruise the head of the serpent.

Jesus came not only to forgive sin, but to restore dominion and to establish His Kingdom. "Pray like this," He said. "Thy

kingdom come, Thy will be done *in earth,* as it is in heaven."
God's order in heaven becomes a pattern for the restoration
of our disordered and chaotic world. Healing for the body is a
part of that divine order.

T. J. McCrossan in his classic work, *Bodily Healing and the
Atonement,* gives six powerful reasons why all Christians
should take Christ as the healer of their bodies.[1] I would like
to recount them here for you.

*Reason One: God used to heal the sick, and He is an un-
changing God.* Throughout the Old and New Testaments we
meet a God who intervenes in times of sickness and pain. The
Bible is about a God of miracles, and healing testimony and
promise abounds from Genesis to Revelation (see Exodus
15:26; 23:25; Psalm 103:3; 105:37; 107:20; Matthew 9:35;
Mark 6:12–13). The Bible also gives no indication that God
would change in some future dispensation. The Word affirms
that He is immutable (Malachi 3:6; James 1:17), and that
Jesus Christ is the same yesterday, today, and forever (Hebrews 13:8).

In the Old Testament God revealed Himself through a
number of special redemptive names:

Jehovah-shammah	The Lord Ever-Present
Jehovah-jireh	The Lord Our Provider
Jehovah-nissi	The Lord Our Banner
Jehovah-shalom	The Lord Our Peace
Jehovah-raah	The Lord My Shepherd
Jehovah-tsidkenu	The Lord Our Righteousness
Jehovah-rapha	The Lord That Healeth Thee

None would deny that God is unchanging in any aspect of
His revealed being, yet some Christians will accept all of

these redemptive names of God, *except the last*. But this is a mighty promise: "I am the Lord that healeth thee [*Jehovah-rapha*]" (Exodus 15:26).

Reason Two: Healing is in the atonement. This means that healing for the body is included in the finished work of Christ's death and resurrection. Isaiah 53, perhaps the greatest messianic prophecy in the Bible, provides a foundation for our understanding of Christ's death. "Surely he hath *borne* our *griefs*, and *carried* our *sorrows*" (verse 4). Note the four key words *italicized* in this verse.

(1) "Griefs" is the Hebrew term *kholee*, which means sickness, and is so translated in Deuteronomy 7:15:

> And the Lord will take away from thee all sickness [*kholee*], and will put none of the evil diseases of Egypt, which thou knowest, upon thee. . . .

(2) "Sorrows" is the Hebrew term *makob*, which means pain as in Jeremiah 51:8:

> Babylon is suddenly fallen and destroyed: howl for her; take balm for her pain [*makob*], if so be she may be healed.

(3) "Borne" is the Hebrew term *nasa*, which means to bear in the sense of suffering punishment for something. This is the connotation in Leviticus 5:1:

> And if a soul sin, and hear the voice of swearing, and is a witness, whether he hath seen or known of it; if he do not utter it, then he shall bear [*nasa*] his iniquity.

(4) "Carried" is the Hebrew term *sabal*, which means "to bear something as a penalty or chastisement." This is the meaning of the word as it is used in Isaiah 53:11:

He shall see of the travail of his soul, and shall be satisfied: by
his knowledge shall my righteous servant justify many; for he
shall bear [*sabal*] their iniquities.

Other translations of the Scriptures affirm that the suffering Messiah would bear our sickness and pains (as well as
our sins) on the cross. Both the Revised Standard Version and
the American Standard Version use the term *sickness*, and
the *Amplified Bible* reads, "Surely he hath borne our griefs—
sickness, weakness and distress—and carried our sorrows *and*
pain." The translation of the Rotherham *Emphasized Bible* is
comparable: "Yet surely our sicknesses he carried, and as for
our pains, he bore the burdens of them."[2]

Listen to what some great men of the faith have had to say
about this passage in Isaiah 53. Alexander McClaren wrote:

> It is to be kept in view, that the griefs, which the Servant
> [Christ] is here described as bearing, are literally sicknesses,
> and that similarly, the sorrows may be diseases. Matthew in
> his quotation of this verse (Matthew 8:17) takes the words to
> refer to bodily ailments; and that interpretation is part of the
> whole truth, for Hebrew thought drew no such sharp line of
> distinction between diseases of the body, and those of the
> soul, as we are accustomed to draw. All sickness was taken to
> be the consequence of sin. . . . Of these two words expressing
> the Servant's taking their burden on His shoulders (*nasa* and
> *sabal*), the former implies not only the taking of it, but the
> bearing of it away; and the latter emphasized the weight of
> the load.[3]

Keil and Delitzsch, recognized as among the foremost Old
Testament scholars, wrote:

> Freely but faithfully does the Gospel of Matthew translate
> this text, "Himself took our infirmities and carried our sick-

nesses." The help which Jesus rendered in all kinds of bodily sickness is taken in Matthew to be a fulfillment of what in Isaiah is prophesied of the Servant of Jehovah. The Hebrew verbs of the text, when used of sin, signify to assume as a heavy burden and bear away the guilt of sin, as one's own; that is, to bear sin mediatorially in order to atone for it. But here, where not our sins, but our sicknesses and pains are the object, the mediatorial sense remains the same. It is not meant that the Servant of Jehovah merely entered into the fellowship of our sufferings, but that he took upon Himself the sufferings that we had to bear, and deserved to bear; and, therefore, He not only bore them away, but also in His own person endured them in order to discharge us from them. Now when one takes sufferings upon himself which another had to bear, and does this, not merely in fellowship with him, but in his stead, we call it Substitution.[4]

Andrew Murray, known for his classic books on the devotional life of the believer, wrote:

It is not said only that the Lord's righteous Servant had borne our sins, but also that He has borne our sicknesses. Thus his bearing our sicknesses forms an integral part of the Redeemer's work, as well as bearing our sins. The body and the soul have been created to serve together as a habitation of God: the sickly condition of the body is—as well as that of the soul—a consequence of sin, and that is what Jesus is come to bear, to expiate and to conquer.[5]

Finally, A. B. Simpson was persuaded that

therefore as He hath borne our sins, Jesus Christ has also borne away, and carried off our sicknesses; yea, and even our pains, so that abiding in Him, we may be fully delivered from both sickness and pain. Thus by His stripes we are healed. Blessed and glorious Burden-Bearer![6]

Perhaps the most convincing argument for the true meaning of Isaiah 53 is found in the New Testament itself.

> When the even was come, they brought unto him many that were possessed with devils: and he cast out the spirits with his word, and healed all that were sick: That it might be fulfilled which was spoken by Esaias the prophet, saying, Himself took our infirmities, and bare our sicknesses.
>
> Matthew 8:16–17

> Who his own self bare our sins in his own body on the tree, that we, being dead to sins, should live unto righteousness: by whose stripes *ye were healed.*   1 Peter 2:24

Another great reference to the price Jesus paid for our healing is found in 1 Corinthians 6:19–20. Here Paul tells us that we have been bought with a price. We have been redeemed by the blood of Christ. Yet, surprisingly, the context here points to the redemption of our *bodies!* "Know ye not that your *body* is the temple of the Holy Ghost . . . and ye are not your own? *For ye are bought with a price:* therefore glorify God *in your body,* and in your spirit, which are God's." Not only has Jesus paid the price for the redemption of our souls; He has also purchased the deliverance of our bodies.

Reason Three: All sickness is the result of Satan's work, and Christ came to destroy the works of the devil. John Wimber has pointed out that there is no fundamental difference between the words and the works of Jesus. They are mutually inclusive. Jesus came not only to preach the gospel of the Kingdom, but also to *do* the will of the Father. "Jesus answered them, I told you, and ye believed not: the works that I do in my Father's name, they bear witness of me" (John

10:25). The words and the works of Jesus are inseparable. To study only the words of Jesus, to isolate His teaching from His miracle ministry, is to misunderstand His mission.

Jesus constantly affirmed His calling by pointing to His .miracles. He demonstrated His authority over Satan by casting out demons; He demonstrated His power over sickness by healing the infirm; and He proved the right to forgive sins on the basis of His miracles (Mark 2:9–11). Peter reported to the household of Cornelius "how God anointed Jesus of Nazareth with the Holy Ghost and with power: who went about doing good, and healing all that were oppressed of the devil" (Acts 10:38).

Certainly, the "worst" work of the devil is sin and its greatest consequence death, particularly the death of the soul. But sickness and pain are also his work, and although most sicknesses are not caused by a specific demon of infirmity, there is no question but that sickness and pain are the direct result of Satan's successful temptation of Adam and Eve. (Note: Approximately one-third of the healings recorded in the Gospels involved exorcism; the other two-thirds were healings from "natural" illnesses.)

Sickness is *not* the will of God, any more than any other aspect of the curse is the will of God. The purpose of the Son of God was to destroy the works of the devil (1 John 3:8), and those works include anything that is not in harmony with heaven. Listen again to the Lord's commission to pray: "Thy kingdom come, Thy will be done in *earth*, as it is in heaven." Listen again to the Great Commission: "All power is given unto me in heaven *and in earth*. Go ye therefore. . . ." The Church has focused all her attention and energies on "Go," and has neglected the very basis of the Commission: the authority of Christ *in the earth*. Jesus came not only to forgive sin and restore the inner man, but also to restore man's dominion over the natural and spiritual worlds, thereby establishing His Kingdom *in the earth*.

For centuries it has been popular among believers to refer to some sickness or infirmity as "the will of God." "Heal me," I pray, *"if it be thy will."* Jesus *never* suggests this view. His words and His works are always consistent: It is the Father's will to bring healing to the oppressed. Those who deny that healing is God's will are consistently inconsistent. If someone really believes it is God's will for him to be sick, why does he take medication, or see a doctor? If he really believes his illness is God's will, then to have surgery to remove a cancer is nothing less than an outright rejection of that will! If it is God's will for me to be sick, I had better not interfere by alleviating my pain and suffering by some artificial means. This, by the way, was the official position of the Church in earlier centuries. The clergyman was called to discern if a person was suffering as the result of some sin in his life, *before* the individual was permitted to see a doctor, as if the sickness might be a punishment sent from God and not meant to be healed.

If on the other hand I believe it is God's will for me to be whole, I have the right both to pray for healing and to see a doctor. And, in fact, even my body, fearfully and wonderfully created by God, testifies that sickness and death are unnatural. If my skin suffers the slightest abrasion, blood rushes to the wound and a fabulous healing process begins. Self-repair is built into my being, and my body struggles to stay alive, resisting the invasion of unfriendly parasites, bonding broken bones and fighting even death itself. Everything in me, physically and emotionally, screams: "I am made for health and life, not sickness and death."

Reason Four: The very same Holy Spirit who was the power behind all of Christ's miracles, and who raised Him from the dead, is still in the Church. Even though Church history witnessed a decline in the frequency of supernatural manifestations, there is no indication in the pages of Scripture that this should have happened. To the contrary, the Bible assumes that the miracle-working power of God is an "ordinary" aspect of Church life. The Holy Spirit of the book of Acts is still present in the Church.

The apostle Paul writes of the Spirit in connection with the life and health of our physical bodies: "But if the Spirit of him that raised up Jesus from the dead dwell in you, he that raised up Christ from the dead shall also quicken [make alive] your mortal bodies by his Spirit that dwelleth in you" (Romans 8:11). The context of Romans 8 persuades us that this is not a reference to the final resurrection, but instead points to the power of the Spirit giving life and strength to my physical body—on this side of heaven. John Calvin wrote, "The quickening of the mortal body here cannot refer to the resurrection of the saints, but must mean a giving of life to their bodies, while here upon the earth, through the Spirit."[7]

Reason Five: Jesus came not only to forgive sin and to save souls, but also to restore dominion. What has been known traditionally as the Great Commission is in fact the Great Recommission. God's original commission is found in the first chapter of the first book of the Bible: "And God said, Let us make man in our image, after our likeness: *and let them have dominion*" (Genesis 1:26). The essential purpose of man is repeated in Psalm 8, where David asks the ageless question, "What is man?" His answer: "Thou madest him *to have dominion* over the works of thy hands; thou has put all things under his feet" (verse 6). Man was created to have dominion, which was tragically relinquished at the Fall.

Hence Jesus' Great *Re*commission: "*All power* is given unto me in heaven *and in earth.* Go ye therefore ..."

(Matthew 28:18–19). The Church has traditionally emphasized *go* and the subsequent preaching, teaching, and baptiz-
ing while virtually ignoring the fountainhead of ministry.
The *go* of the Great Commission is meaningless without the
basis of Christ's authority and power *in the earth*. This is the
consistent emphasis of all the Great Recommission passages:

> Go ye into the world, and preach the gospel to every crea-
> ture. ... And these signs shall follow them that believe; In
> my name shall they cast out devils; they shall speak with new
> tongues; They shall take up serpents; and if they drink any
> deadly thing, it shall not hurt them; they shall lay hands on
> the sick, and they shall recover.... And they went forth, and
> preached every where, the Lord working with them, and
> confirming the word with signs following.
>
> Mark 16:15, 17–18, 20

Some may argue, "This last portion of Mark is not found in
all of the ancient manuscripts." This is true, but it does not
lessen the importance of the message. First, there are sound
reasons for accepting this passage as genuine. Very recent
textual research has brought new light to the much maligned
Byzantine Text-Type, the ancient source of these verses.[8]
Second, even if we reject the text as spurious, this reading
shows that the early Church saw miracles in connection with
the Great Commission. Third, all the other Great Commission passages speak of authority, dominion, and power:

> Then opened he their understanding ... And said unto
> them, Thus it is written ... that repentance and remission of
> sins should be preached in his name among all nations, begin-
> ning at Jerusalem. And ye are witnesses of these things. And,
> behold, I send the promise of my Father upon you: but tarry

ye in the city of Jerusalem, *until ye be endued with power
from on high.*   Luke 24:45–49

But ye shall receive power, after that the Holy Ghost is come
upon you.   Acts 1:8

The personal training the disciples received in preparation
for their ministry affirms the miracle aspect of the Great
Commission. When Jesus sent out the twelve and later the
seventy, He charged them to preach the gospel *and to heal
the sick.* It is unimaginable that Jesus would train His followers for miracle ministry, that He would send their faith soar-
ing, only to strip them of that ministry at His ascension.
What He commanded at His final departure was simply an
extension of His words and works, which He had taught them
so carefully and diligently. To be released into power ministry was a graduation, so to speak, after Jesus' followers
completed their program of training in His school of disci-
pleship.

And Jesus went about all the cities and villages, teaching in
their synagogues, and preaching the gospel of the kingdom,
*and healing every sickness and every disease among the peo-
ple.*   Matthew 9:35

Then he called his twelve disciples together, and gave *them
power and authority over all devils, and to cure diseases.* And
he sent them to preach the kingdom of God, and *to heal the
sick.* [See Matthew 10:1, 7–8; Mark 3:14–15; 6:7, 13.]
                                                  Luke 9:1–2;

After these things the Lord appointed other seventy also,
and sent them two and two before his face into every city and

place, whither he himself would come. Therefore said he unto them . . . *heal the sick* . . . and say unto them, The kingdom of God is come nigh unto you. Luke 10:1–2, 9

James is in perfect harmony with the Great Commission when He charges the elders to pray for the sick. Technically, it is the sick person who is being commissioned to appeal to the elders: "Is any sick among you? let him call for the elders of the church; and let them pray over him, anointing him with oil in the name of the Lord: And the prayer of faith shall save the sick, and the Lord shall raise him up" (James 5:14–15).

I was traveling and ministering in Eastern Europe recently, and became acquainted with a young Christian medical doctor who was wrestling with questions about healing. After a couple of hours of talking about it, it occurred to me to tell him that I pray for the sick because the Bible commands it, not because I understand it fully, or because it always "works." Quite suddenly he was completely satisfied, and our discussion of healing ended abruptly. If for no other reason, healing is God's will because healing is God's command. If God has commissioned us to pray for the sick, then it must be God's will to heal us.

Reason Six: Healing is one of God's marvelous promises. We are encouraged by the Scriptures to believe God for virtually everything. Listen to these comprehensive promises:

And whatsoever we ask, we receive of him, because we keep his commandments. 1 John 3:22

Have faith in God. . . . What things soever ye desire, when ye pray, believe that ye receive them, and ye shall have them. Mark 11:22, 24

My God shall supply all your need according to his riches in glory by Christ Jesus.   Philippians 4:19

His divine power hath given unto us all things that pertain unto life and godliness.   2 Peter 1:3

All the promises of God in him [Christ] are yea, and in him Amen, unto the glory of God by us.   2 Corinthians 1:20

Whoever we ask, we receive—except healing for our bodies?

What things we desire, we receive—except healing for our bodies?

God shall supply all our need—except healing for our bodies?

He has given us all things—except healing for our bodies?

All the promises are yea—except healing for our bodies?

Everything except healing? A thousand times, No!

Chapter Eighteen

Why Doesn't God Always Heal?

IF IT IS GOD'S WILL for us to be healed, why are so many Christians still sick after prayer? This question haunts people who believe in healing, and it is a common objection of those who do not.

Hundreds of books and pamphlets have been written and countless sermons have been preached in response to this issue, which tells me that there are more questions than there are answers. The answer is not simple, regardless of how simply some healing ministries seem to present the matter. Healing is the will of God for His people, but healing cannot be reduced to a mere formula. My premise for understanding this difficult and sensitive issue is 1 Corinthians 8:2: "If any man think that he knoweth any thing, he knoweth nothing yet as he ought to know." Later in his same letter Paul writes, "We know *in part*" (13:9). But even though we have limited knowledge, we can try to understand this question of healing.

I have heard several reasons expressed why people are not healed. Perhaps the most common response to the question,

144

"Why am I still sick?" is unbelief, or as so many have termed it, "a lack of faith." This response has both positive and negative aspects.

Positively, the Scriptures are unmistakably clear when they tell us that "without faith it is impossible to please [God]" (Hebrews 11:6). James affirms the essentialness of faith in his spiritual prescription for healing: "The prayer *of faith* shall save the sick" (James 5:15). Numerous are the examples of healing "by faith" in the Gospels. More often than not personal faith is the avenue of miracles (see Matthew 8:5–13; 15:28; 17:14–21; Luke 9:40–42; 17:19; John 4:46–54; 11:22). To deny this is to reject a major aspect of New Testament revelation: The promises of God are accessible to those who believe.

This does not mean, however, that we are entitled to expect answers on faith alone. We must also *ask* for healing, and not think: "If God wants me to have it, I will get it whether or not I do anything about it." This idea, as I have said earlier, is entirely foreign to the teaching of the New Testament, inclusive of tongues, healing, the spiritual gifts, and even salvation itself. Earnestly "desire the spiritual gifts," Paul commands (1 Corinthians 14:1), and "Pray for one another, that ye might be healed," says James, because "the effectual *fervent* prayer of a righteous man availeth much" (James 5:16). To illustrate, James points us to Elijah who "prayed *earnestly*" (verse 17).

There was a time in my life when I was ignorant of the fact that healing for my body was a promise of God's Word, so I never prayed for healing for myself or anyone else. And guess what? I never saw myself or anyone else healed! Admittedly, God heals sovereignly, and there are examples of that in the Bible (John 5:1–9), but I could not then testify with the apostle Peter, "And his name, *through faith* in his name, hath made this man strong" (Acts 3:16). However, when I began to recognize that God heals the sick in answer to our prayers, and when I began to pray and believe, people were healed.

I am not blind to the fact that many I pray for are not healed, but many are. Some are healed through my faith; no one is healed through unbelief or ignorance. Even the Son of God Himself, as we are told in one of the most remarkable and mystifying passages of the Bible, was not able to work miracles because of community unbelief (Matthew 13:58; Mark 6:5–6).

One objection often leads to another, and, unfortunately, the "negative" aspect of a "lack of faith" often enters here: If faith is the key to possessing the promises of God, and I am not healed when I pray, does this mean that I do not have enough faith?

It is here we come face-to-face with a crisis of theological logic that has brought spiritual and emotional trauma to countless believers. It has led them to question their personal faith and even the character of God. It has also resulted in the rejection of medical treatment for themselves and their families. We have all heard the horror stories of children who have died because their parents "in faith" have withheld medication or medical treatment.

Faith is a master key, but faith is not the whole counsel of God. If we are not careful, the message of faith can become a subtle form of legalism. Faith, in effect, becomes a "work" upon which the blessing of God depends. Faith works, but faith is not a work. I am not healed by my faith, but by God who is the Object of my faith. Legalism is the result of a wrong view of faith, and spiritual pride is the child of legalism.

This same balance, of doing our part and trusting God to do His also, surfaces in another commonly expressed reason why people are not healed: sin. Again we find that the Bible often makes a connection between sin and sickness (Deuteronomy 28; 2 Kings 5:20–27; 1 Corinthians 11:29–30; John 5:5–14; 9:1–3; Luke 1:20; Acts 5:1–11; 13:11). Watchman Nee has written, "So far as mankind is concerned, sickness *does* come from sin; but in relation to the *individual* it may or may not be the case." It has been verified by medical and psychological research that wrong attitudes like anger and bitterness can have a direct and frightening affect on a person's physical body.

Sin is undeniably a cause of sickness, generally and individually, but like faith, it must *not* become my focus. I must continue to remind myself that Jesus died to forgive me and to deliver me from my sin, and if salvation is a free gift by grace through faith then healing must be too!

I was once approached by a woman who had had a long and difficult battle with a minor illness. She told me she "had tried everything," but still was not healed. I finally asked: "Have you 'tried' trusting Jesus? After all, your healing is based on what He has done, not on what you do." Her face came alive with joy as this scriptural counsel liberated her from false guilt, and within a short time she was completely whole.

Another cause of sickness and continued poor health is improper nutrition and a lack of exercise. I suppose that this could even be considered an aspect of sin, since it involves a violation of God's natural laws of good food and good rest. Our bodies, we are told, are temples of the Holy Spirit, and as such require our special attention and care (see 1 Corinthians 6:19–20).

Why are people not healed? Unbelief, sin, and bad nutrition. A good biblical case can be made for all three, but is this enough? Is there something we are further called to understand? I believe so. It is related to our attitudes. Allow me to suggest a biblical directive that I think can help lift the clouds of misunderstanding enshrouding the promise of healing, and guide us in our response to unanswered prayer.

The Great Contradiction

Thou has put all things in subjection under his [man's] feet.
For in that he put all in subjection under him, he left nothing
that is not put under him. But now we see not yet all things
put under him. But we see Jesus. . . .   Hebrews 2:8–9

In this single verse we have a statement and an explanation of the great contradiction of the Christian life, the ambiguity of what is, and what ought to be. Solomon wrote: ". . . The race is not to the swift, nor the battle to the strong, neither yet bread to the wise, nor yet riches to men of understanding, nor yet favor to men of skill; but time and chance happeneth to them all" (Ecclesiastes 9:11). The question for us is: If God's Word is true, why doesn't it always work?

In Jesus, we see fully what ought to be (that is, the "not yet"). He is the revelation of God and His purpose for man. When Jesus entered ministry, He prayed for the sick, cast out devils, and raised the dead. Furthermore, the apostles were commissioned on several occasions to continue this ministry of supernatural power. That they did so is recorded in the book of Acts.

If the Church, the Body of Christ on this earth, is to be a full expression of His character and power, then miracles should happen. Indeed, they should be expected. Jesus left His disciples with this sure hope when He declared, "All power is given unto me in heaven and in earth. Go ye therefore . . ." (Matthew 28:18–19). If Christ is the fullness of God to us, and we are the fullness of Christ to the world, then we can believe that divine healing for the body is God's "perfect" will.

Yet what God's Word promises, and what we see with our natural senses, often contradict one another. We pray, and people are not healed. Using the analogy of sin, the same thing occurs. In God's Word, we see the promise of deliverance from sin, even that all of our sins have already been taken away as far as the East is from the West. We rejoice! And keep right on sinning. (Some have deluded themselves into thinking they have actually stopped.) We are faced with the same tension between what ought to be and what is.

All things have been put in subjection to Christ—*all things*—but we do not yet see all things in subjection to Him. Many times people simply are not healed. What do we do in that situation? We see Jesus . . . who hung right there on the Cross and died; the Great Physician, who did not heal Himself; who walked with the Father in incredibly intimate communion, but said in His dying breath, "My God, My God [not My Father], why have You forsaken Me?" We see Jesus, who has felt the contradiction between what is and what ought to be, the "now" and the "not yet," more than anyone. He is our High Priest, touched by the feeling of our infirmities—our moments, years of helplessness. I don't always understand why, *but I see Jesus.*

Even if Jesus does not seem to exercise His Lordship and change circumstances, even when those circumstances contradict His Word, He is still Lord of my responses to those things, if I allow Him to be. The wonderful declaration that "Jesus is Lord" is not a magic wand for me to wave over every situation that makes me feel uncomfortable. "Jesus is Lord" means that He is in control of me and how I react emotionally and attitudinally to situations I do not like. "Offenses must come," Jesus said (Matthew 18:7), but by His Spirit He is working in me the right responses to those offenses. Prayer changes things, but it changes me the most. Jesus is Lord of my character development and the final outcome of every circumstance (Romans 8:28).

It is God's will to heal . . . and to save . . . and to deliver . . . and to prosper His people . . . and to establish justice in the earth. It does not always happen. Now we do not yet see all things in subjection to Him, but we see Jesus! He is our example of hope and persistent faith.

Look at Jesus. Based on God's Word, He Himself prays for me constantly (Hebrews 7:25). His Spirit prays for me, too, and His prayers are always right "because he maketh intercession for the saints according to the will of God" (Romans 8:27). Consider this thought: If healing is the will of God, and the Spirit prays according to God's will, does this mean that even the Spirit does not get His prayers answered immediately? Even Jesus, in His intercession, is caught in the tension between what is and what ought to be, the "now" and the "not yet." For example, He prayed for the Church to be one (John 17:21), and yet this prayer is still waiting to be answered. Now we do not yet see the Church as one.

There is a liberating lesson here about faith, as we watch how Jesus Himself responds to "unanswered" prayer. Our Lord is faithful to pray, no matter what happens. His faith in God's will never falters. He persistently presses toward the moment when every knee shall bow and every enemy shall be brought under His authority and control (1 Corinthians 15:25). He never stops praying God's Word, and He does not blame Himself when God's Word is not immediately fulfilled.

In striking contrast, how do we usually respond when our prayers are not answered? We either give up and, in effect, blame God, saying, "It must not be God's will for me," even though it is in His Word. Or we begin to blame ourselves and incur false guilt, wondering, "Is it the way I pray? My lack of faith? Is something wrong with me?"

When my prayers do not change things I must look to Jesus, who is the author *and finisher* of my faith (Hebrews 12:2), and when I "see Jesus," He becomes my example of how I should respond to unanswered prayer: I must keep pressing forward to the fulfillment of God's Word and promise.

Is healing God's will? Yes—it is a Kingdom promise; it is what is coming. But if a person is not healed now, it means that the sickness is not yet subject to him. This, however, does not mean I accept the now as final. "Now" only lasts an instant before it disappears into the past. Even though I am not healed now, I may be in the very next moment! So I can keep right on believing.

All of this is somewhat like the Second Coming of Christ. Jesus is coming anytime, but if He does not come now, in the immediate moment, I don't give up. I keep right on expecting Him. Similarly, if I am not healed, I do not give up and resign myself to the sickness, thinking that it is God's will. I just keep right on praying and believing. Ever take a long trip with kids? Mine ask constantly, "When are we going to get there?" It seems that a parent's most common response is, "We're *almost* there."

Even when a Christian dies, our hope is not quenched. For the Christian there is never an "end," a time to give up and say, "Things will never change. Therefore, this must be God's will for me." The promise of God is always in front of us. We are constantly moving toward a goal, and we are always "almost there." "Be thou faithful [keep on being faithful, persist in faith] unto [as far as] death, and I will give thee a crown of life" (Revelation 2:10).

Faith (or faithfulness) becomes the primary principle of the Kingdom of God. "Faith is the substance of things hoped for" (Hebrews 11:1). Faith brings the promise (the not yet) into the present (the now). Even if the thing hoped for is still hoped for, faith keeps on keeping on. Faith *is*. Now we do not yet see all things in subjection to Him, *but we see Jesus*. "Consider him that endured such contradiction of sinners against himself, lest ye be wearied and faint in your minds" (Hebrews 12:3).

To summarize: (1) Healing is God's will. You can keep believing for it, no matter how it looks *now*. No matter how dim the doctor's report becomes, it always remains God's will for you to be healed. (2) Just because you are not healed immediately does not reflect some failure on your part, any more than it reflects failure on the part of the Lord Jesus Himself. It is a simple fact of this age: *Now* we do *not yet* see all things subject to Him, but the fulfillment of the promise is always around the corner. We are always "almost there."

Chapter Nineteen

Inner Healing

INNER HEALING, which may also be called the healing of the soul, or the healing of memories, is a legitimate expression of the ministry of the Holy Spirit. It is a releasing and cleansing of the inner life. We return to the great prophecy of Isaiah 53. Included in the all-sufficient work of our Savior was the "chastisement of our peace" (Isaiah 53:5). The *Amplified Bible* reads, "The chastisement needful to obtain peace and well-being for us was upon Him."

Somehow, it has been easy for us to accept great theological implications of Christ's ministry, like the peace with God that accompanies justification. But often, practical aspects of the ministry of reconciliation are not emphasized, like peace within our own being. "Be anxious for nothing," Paul commands. Anxiety is the archenemy of peace. "But in every thing . . . with thanksgiving let your requests be made known unto God. And the peace of God, which passeth all understanding, shall keep your hearts and minds [guard your emotions and thoughts] through Christ Jesus" (Philippians 4:6-7).

When Jesus died on the Cross, He was bruised for our sins, for our physical sicknesses and pains, and for our emotional traumas: Jesus died for the wholeness of our whole being. The apostle Paul wrote, "And the very God of peace sanctify you *wholly:* and I pray God your *whole* spirit and soul and body be preserved blameless unto the coming of our Lord Jesus Christ" (1 Thessalonians 5:23). Jesus came to bring the order of God, the Kingdom, into the disorder and chaos of our world, and He has sent us on the same mission: "As thou hast sent me into the world, even so have I also sent them into the world" (John 17:18).

Isaiah 53 provides the basis for the healing of the inner man: the finished work of Christ. James 5:15 points to its practice: the prayer of faith. After promising that prayer and anointing would heal sick bodies, James adds, "Confess your faults one to another, and pray one for another, that ye may be healed" (James 5:16). On the surface, this verse is teaching that there is a relationship between psychology and physical health, a fact verified by contemporary medical and psychological research. James also implies, however, that the healing of the inner life is necessary as well, something that may be just as dramatic as physical healing. Some individuals have spiritual bondages and psychological strongholds that can be broken only by the power of God's Spirit. Perhaps this is the most outstanding aspect of inner healing—the sudden supernatural release of God's power to bring deliverance and emotional healing.

Paul understands this when he says: "For the weapons of our warfare are not carnal, but mighty [*dunamis*] through God to the pulling down of strongholds" (2 Corinthians 10:4).

The next verse identifies these strongholds: imaginations and other fortresses of the mind. Every thought must be brought out of the captivity of the past and under the dominion of Christ. The battleground is the mind, the stronghold of memories and distorted perceptions.

I am not psychologizing the New Testament. I am, in fact, spiritualizing it. Paul himself is teaching that the solution to man's problem is a spiritual one—"We do not war after the flesh." Though we walk in the flesh, though the root of our problem is in our fleshly imagination, we do not fight flesh with flesh, psychological problems with psychological solutions. Instead, we pull down strongholds with the weapons of the Spirit. Inner healing is nothing more, and nothing less, than the wielding of the weapons of the Spirit, using supernatural solutions to solve natural problems.

Simply stated, inner healing is the operation of the gifts of the Holy Spirit in the counseling session. For some years now, the supernatural gifts of the Holy Spirit have been a common feature of public church services in charismatic churches. More recently, however, this phenomenon of inner healing has been experienced by individual believers in one-on-one counseling and prayer ministry. Inner healing is the exercise of the gifts of the Spirit in personal ministry. It is counseling under the anointing.

The phenomenon known as inner healing has two goals. Its primary and spiritual objective is to extend the Lordship and healing power of Christ into our past history, affecting even our pre-conversion experience. Its secondary and psychological goal is thereby to release us from whatever emotional and psychological bondage our past experience has produced. Inner healing theorists claim that emotional blocks and habitual behavior patterns (with their negative fruits of frustration, defeat and poor self-image) prevent us from moving into the abundant life that Jesus promised. Therefore, they conclude, a special effort should be made to heal these inner wounds, so that we may be free from the many ways in which they constrict and impoverish our lives. In summary, the overall goal of inner healing can be described as a kind of "retroactive sanctification."[1]

Some Questions

Does everyone need inner healing? Yes and no. If we think of inner healing as the restoration and renewal of the soul (*psyche*, that is, personality), then the answer is yes. We all need cleansing from the unrighteousness of the flesh (1 John 1:8). Inner healing may take place in a quiet, unspectacular way when people hear and are set free by the proclamation of the Word (John 17:17).

On the other hand, inner healing as a dramatic deliverance session is not for everyone. Like Paul, some have sudden and powerful encounters with the Lord. Like Timothy, some do not. In this sense, inner healing is not a panacea, a cure-all, and should be viewed as only one aspect of personal ministry.

Is inner healing a counseling technique? My answer is no. True, a person can learn how to minister inner healing, but it is not simply a counseling "technique." We find a parallel in the story of the sons of the high priest who tried to cast out a spirit "in the name of the Jesus that Paul preaches" (Acts 19:13–16). The consequences were disastrous. Inner healing that has degenerated to a mere technique may not be much different than New Age self-help. Inner healing is not a static formula; it is the creative and spontaneous power of the Holy Spirit operating through the believer (John 3:8).

What about imaging? Without prayer for the guidance of the Holy Spirit and reliance on the Word, creating mental images can be a pathway to deception. A. W. Tozer rightly warned of "idols of the mind." However, the Bible is full of symbols, parables, and imagery, and we are instructed, "Whatsoever things are true ... honest ... just ... pure ... lovely ... of good report ... virtuous ... praiseworthy ... *think on these things*" (Philippians 4:8). Psalm 23 is a classic example of Old Testament imagery, a source of immeasurable comfort to countless believers. Is it permissible for us to "think on these things"—still waters and pastures green? I think so. Can I picture in my mind Jesus taking the little children in His arms? I think so. May I imagine Jesus taking *me* into His arms? Yes!

The Lord may also use dreams, visions, and mental pictures to reveal Himself and to bring healing. The critical issue is whether the persons involved in the inner healing process are using psychic power to create the image or whether the power of the Holy Spirit is creating the image through the living Word. It is the Word of God that divides between soul (*psyche*) and spirit.

I am also comforted by the promise that if I ask for the Holy Spirit, God will not release a demon in my life (Luke 11:10–13). I *must* trust that the Word and the Spirit will sanctify my meditation. The psalmist prayed confidently, "Let the words of my mouth, and the meditation of my heart, be acceptable in thy sight, O, Lord, my strength, and my redeemer" (Psalm 19:14). This implies two things. First, it is possible for my meditations to be unacceptable. Second, if I delight myself in the Lord, He will give me the desires (meditations) of my heart.

Loren Sanford writes:

We are called to prophesy not from our own minds and hearts, but from the Spirit of God. Occult healers often make things happen by visualizing them into reality. By contrast, Christian healers prophesy things into reality. The prophet speaks forth for God that which God has commanded him to speak. The difference is that the Christian healer is constrained to speak or to describe only the vision given him by the Lord, never the vision he, in his own flesh, would like to see, no matter how kind or apparently necessary that vision may seem. We work by spiritual gifts of perception, discernment and prophetic word, but never by technique bordering on magic.

In short, if we would remain within the safe boundaries of the eternal word of God, we must confine ourselves to the simple pattern of confession, repentance, forgiveness, the fatherhood of God and the gifts of the Spirit which enable us to discern the hearts of men, and to speak the healing word. We must avoid those approaches to counseling which copy the techniques of psychic healers and other "New Age" deceivers. There is a world of difference between visualizing and receiving a vision. We must seek as best we can to be certain that what we see in praying for inner healing is from God by the Holy Spirit and therefore reflective of what He is doing. Likewise, we must avoid visualizing from our own hearts and minds by acts of the human will. As for me, I am constrained to limit myself to describing the vision the Lord gives prophetically in the moment. By this God truly heals. And this is not a method. This is obedience.[2]

Where does caution about inner healing stop, and paranoia begin? Caution and discernment are essential in any spiritual ministry. The biblical warning is clear: "Let him that thinketh he standeth take heed lest he fall" (1 Corinthians 10:12), and "If any man think that he knoweth anything, he knoweth nothing yet as he ought to know" (1 Corinthians 8:2). We must persist in doing what we feel is right, while at the same time openly confessing our propensity for error. I pursue excellence, but every word and work must be judged by the Scriptures and by the brethren.

Yet Jesus said something that brings great relief to my soul: "When you have done your very best, you are still unprofitable servants" (Luke 17:10, my paraphrase). This is certainly not an excuse for mediocrity, but it is a source of comfort. When Paul's apostolic authority was being questioned, his response was, "But with me it is a very small thing that I should be judged of you, or of man's judgment; yea, I judge not mine own self . . . but he that judgeth me is the Lord. Therefore judge nothing before the time, until the Lord come, who both will bring to light the hidden things of darkness, and will make manifest the counsels of the hearts; *and then shall every man have praise* [not condemnation] *from God*" (1 Corinthians 4:3–5). The criterion for successful ministry is faithfulness, not errorlessness.

There is safety in the multitude of counselors, but ultimately I must answer to God. Caution, wisdom, humility, discernment—these are all necessary aspects of sound ministry. But when these virtues evolve subtly into an inquisitional paranoia about inner healing—or any other aspect of the Holy Spirit's work—then we are in danger of becoming just as deceived as if we were teaching false doctrine. History tells us plainly and horribly that fanaticism for an absolute religious purity can have a destructive force equal to, perhaps greater than, outright deception. Solomon warns, "Be not righteous over much, neither make thyself over wise: why shouldest thou destroy thyself?" (Ecclesiastes 7:16). We can be so right that we are wrong. Caution and discernment? Yes. Paranoia? No, for we have not been given a spirit of fear, but of love—covenantal commitment to one another. And perfect love casts out all fear.

Chapter Twenty

Prosperity in Perspective

Is PROSPERITY a forgotten truth or a Pandora's box? The debate has been bitter and people have taken sides.

"God wants you rich," claim the "faith" people.

"Believing God for wealth is nothing more than a religious form of American materialism," cry their opponents.

"Poverty syndrome!" is the retort.

"Success at the expense of the poor. Paganism," is the quick reply.

What is the answer? What does the Bible say? What is the "whole counsel of God" on this important issue? The psalmist wrote, "Truth is the total of the full meaning of all Your individual precepts" (Psalm 119:160, *The Amplified Bible*). Is it possible to balance the accounts of prosperity and wealth?

A Theology of Prosperity

Prosperity is not a bad word. It is not only in the Bible, it is even used in a positive sense! God told Joshua that if he gave

161

careful attention to the Word—thinking about it, speaking it, and obeying it—then his way would be prosperous and he would have good success (Joshua 1:8). The psalmist echoes this same idea: "Blessed is the man . . . [whose] delight is in the law of the Lord . . . and whatsoever he doeth shall prosper" (Psalm 1:1, 3). Prosperity is not limited or capped: "*Whatsoever* he doeth shall prosper."

Deuteronomy even suggests that material blessing is an aspect of the covenant God made with Israel. Jehovah warned His people not to say in their hearts, "My power and the might of mine hand hath gotten me this wealth. But thou shalt remember the Lord thy God: for it is he that giveth thee power to get wealth, *that he may establish his covenant* which he sware unto thy fathers" (Deuteronomy 8:17–18).

The Hebrew term translated "wealth" has multiple meanings, but it is clear from the context here that it refers to material things, the milk and honey of the good and rich land. Furthermore, this material blessing is connected to the Abrahamic covenant of promise, not the Mosaic covenant of the Law. The wealth is promised through the covenant that God "sware unto thy fathers," a reference to Abraham, Isaac, and Jacob. Paul writes, "For if the inheritance be of the law, it is no more of promise: but God gave it to *Abraham by promise*" (Galatians 3:18).

Now it is evident from the context of this Scripture that the inheritance of which Paul speaks is the gracious gift of salvation through Jesus Christ. Yet it is also clear that the Abrahamic covenant was an Old Testament forerunner of the new covenant of grace and promise. It was through this covenant, not the covenant of the Law originating at Sinai, that God gave the Israelites their wealth. This inheritance of grace is affirmed in Deuteronomy 9: "Not for thy righteous-ness, or for the uprightness of thine heart, dost thou go to pos-sess their land: but . . . that he may perform the word which the Lord sware unto thy fathers, Abraham, Isaac, and Jacob" (verse 5).

Prosperity and success are common themes in the Old Tes-tament, and though they occur less frequently in the New Testament, they are not entirely absent from the writings of the new covenant.

> And Jesus answered and said, Verily I say unto you, There is no man that hath left house, or brethren, or sisters, or fa-ther, or mother, or wife, or children, or lands, for my sake, and the gospel's, but he shall receive an hundredfold *now in this time,* houses, and brethren, and sisters, and mothers, and children, and lands, with persecutions; and *in the world to come, eternal life.* Mark 10:29–30

Notice the clear distinction between blessings in this life, on the one hand, and on the other hand, eternal life in the world to come. Jesus also promised that if we give freely, then the blessing will be returned to us in abundance, "good measure, pressed down, and shaken together" (Luke 6:38). This is parallel with Proverbs 3:9–10, where we read,

> Honor the Lord with thy substance, and with the firstfruits of all thine increase: So shall thy barns be filled with plenty, and thy presses shall burst out with new wine.

Our expectations as Christians will be determined by our view of God and our understanding of God's Word. The great contribution of the faith/prosperity message is that it has lifted and broadened our view of God. God's people need to realize that we serve a God of abundance, and that He delights in blessing his people. "If ye then, being evil, know how to give good gifts unto your children, how much more shall your Father which is in heaven give good things to them that ask him?" (Matthew 7:11).

The list of the promises of God's rich provision goes on:

> God . . . giveth us richly all things to enjoy.
> 1 Timothy 6:17

> But my God shall supply all your needs according to his riches in glory by Christ Jesus.   Philippians 4:19

> His divine power hath given unto us all things that pertain unto life and godliness [natural life and spiritual life].
> 2 Peter 1:3

> I wish above all things that thou mayest prosper and be in health, even as thy soul prospereth.   3 John 2

The apostle Paul wrote, "I know both how to be abased, and I know how to abound: every where and in all things I am instructed both to be full and to be hungry, both to abound and to suffer need" (Philippians 4:12). The Church has specialized in, if not mastered, the art of being abased. We need a new revelation about how to abound, how to be full, how to prosper without feeling guilty. It is my strong conviction that this must be our starting point for understanding God. Our God is a God of abundance, not restraint, restriction, judgment, and displeasure. Our God delights in blessing his people.

Aside from these many popular prosperity promises, the ministry of Jesus provides a model for understanding God's purposes for us. In the first weeks of His public ministry, Jesus stood up in the synagogue in Nazareth and read from Isaiah 61:

> The Spirit of the Lord is upon me, because he hath anointed me to preach the gospel to the poor; he hath sent me to heal the broken-hearted, to preach deliverance to the captives, and recovering of sight to the blind, to set at liberty them that are bruised.   Luke 4:18

Notice that each phase of the ministry of our Lord is "results"-oriented. His message was not in word only, but in power, to do the things necessary to liberate people from sin and its oppressive consequences.

The "gospel to the poor" is not some injection of religious morphine to enable them to endure their poverty. God forbid! The gospel to the poor is, rather, a message of the Kingdom, a revelation of God's order in a disordered world, a proclamation of justice in the face of injustice, an announcement of dignity and hope *in this life* for those who are hopeless and have no dignity.

I have traveled in ministry in Mexico and Eastern Europe, places of economic deprivation and hopelessness, and I have seen the message of the Kingdom—*the power of the gospel*—change people, give them dignity and hope, and bring them into a place of prosperity and success, perhaps not according to American standards, but then America is not God's standard. My point is that the gospel to the poor must be seen as having a dramatic affect on poverty *in this life*.

I have a friend who is a black pastor serving in an urban ghetto in the Midwest. Giving glory to God, he boasted, "You know of the high unemployment rate among young blacks in America? We do not have *one single* unemployed young person in our large church!" His secret? A revelation to the poor of the gospel of the Kingdom! The Word of God is a source both of instruction for a successful lifestyle and the power to become a new person. "His delight is in the law of the Lord; and in his law doth he meditate day and night . . . and whatsoever he doeth shall prosper"(Psalm 1:2–3).

A Theology of Balance

Our God delights in blessing His people, *provided they keep His provision in perspective*. Proverbs has a great word in this regard: "Remove far from me vanity and lies; give me neither poverty nor riches; feed me with food convenient for me: Lest I be full, and deny thee, and say, Who is the Lord? or lest I be poor, and steal, and take the name of my God in vain" (Proverbs 30:8–9). The promise of prosperity must be kept in balance. The desperately wicked human heart, as Jeremiah calls it, must have its restraints.

The biblical term for balance is "temperance," which Paul lists among the fruit of the Spirit in Galatians 5:23. The Greek word actually means "self-control." Applying this to money, it has been said, "It is not how much money you have, but how much your money has you."

Paul wrote to Timothy: "Charge them that are rich in this world. . . ." Charge them what? Pause and contemplate how many ways this sentence has been completed by well-meaning pastors! Paul does not say what so many might anticipate, like for example, "Charge them that are rich in this world to give it all away." No, Paul instructs Timothy to charge them "that they be not highminded [proud of their wealth], nor trust in uncertain riches, but in the living God." He is telling them, essentially, "Take charge of your money, but don't let it take charge of you."

Prosperity has its limits, and those limits are defined by one, the will of God for each individual and, two, one's personal level of spiritual strength to resist the temptations that accompany wealth. "Ye ask, and receive not," James writes, "because ye ask amiss [out of the will of God], that ye may consume it upon your lusts" (4:3). Faith may be defined as asking for God's abundant provision, within the boundary of His special plan for your life. Presumption is stepping outside that boundary.

Additionally, there are three fundamental principles that help each of us define those boundaries and judge our subtle motives of covetousness. The first is *faithfulness*. Paul writes that stewards must be *faithful* (1 Corinthians 4:1–2). Faith is one side of the prosperity dollar; faithfulness is the other. Only one side of the money says, "In God we trust." That's our starting point. *Unless the Lord builds the house,* we labor in vain. Our source is God Himself and the promise of His provision, but the Scriptures are equally clear that if a person doesn't work, he shouldn't eat either. *We must labor!*

Labor in itself is not vain; it is labor apart from the Lord that is meaningless. "Let him that stole steal no more: but rather let him labor, working with his hands the thing which is good . . ." (Ephesians 4:28). Faith is never a substitute for a lack of labor. Faith must be balanced with hard work, diligence, and good stewardship.

The first guardrail along the chasm of presumption is faithfulness. The second is a good memory:

When thou hast eaten and art full, then thou shalt bless the Lord thy God for the good land which he hath given thee. *Beware that thou forget not* the Lord thy God ... Lest when thou has eaten and art full, and hast built goodly houses ... And when thy herds and thy flocks multiply, and thy silver and thy gold is multiplied, and all that thou hast is multiplied; Then thine heart be lifted up ["highminded" in 1 Timothy 6:17], *and thou forget the Lord thy God. ... But thou shalt remember* the Lord thy God: for it is he that giveth thee power to get wealth. ... And it shall be, if thou do at all *forget* the Lord thy God ... ye shall surely perish.

Deuteronomy 8:10–14, 18–19

Right priorities is another expression for a good memory. Jesus taught us to lay up treasure in heaven, not in the earth, where "moth and rust doth corrupt, and where thieves break through and steal. ... For where your treasure [your *priority*] is, there will your heart be also" (Matthew 6:19–21). Your heart is the measure of your relationship with God, not your treasures. This was most evident in the Laodicean church of Revelation 3:

Thou sayest, I am rich, and increased with goods, and have need of nothing; and knowest not that thou art wretched, and miserable, and poor, and blind, and naked.   Verse 17

The third principle of balance is generosity. Generosity is the antidote for the poison of greed. Giving is both the cause of blessing and the cure for materialism. The mark of true prosperity in a believer's life is his utter willingness to give everything away. This, in fact, is the essence of God's blessing and abundance. God supplies in order to meet our needs. Beyond that, God blesses us so that we can give freely to others. We return to Ephesians 4:

> Let him that stole steal no more: but rather let him labor, working with his hands the thing which is good, *that he may have to give to him that needeth.*   Verse 28

Paul further wrote to Timothy, "Charge them that are rich in this world . . . that they do good, that they be rich in good works . . . willing to communicate" (1 Timothy 6:17–18). The Greek term translated "willing to communicate" means "having something in common." Paul is instructing Timothy to challenge the rich to share the wealth.

Materialism and the Ministry

Perhaps the hardest prosperity pill for Christians to swallow is the abuse of money by prominent leaders in the church. I know of a fairly popular television evangelist who spent over ten thousand dollars remodeling his private office, and he did it with widows' mites. I also knew an elderly, dying widow who faithfully supported this man's ministry with the few dollars she had left after paying for a dingy room in a fourth-class rest home. I know of another pastor of a small congregation who confessed aloud, from his pulpit, every Sunday for better than a year that God would give him a new, plush van for his ministry. Guess what? One of his members finally complied with his confessional brainwashing.

Numerous have been the revelations of abuse and misman-agement of funds in Christian organizations. Perhaps it is a fulfillment of Micah's ancient prophecy:

> The heads thereof judge for reward, and the priests thereof teach for hire, and the prophets thereof divine for money: *yet will they lean upon the Lord, and say, Is not the Lord among us?*   Micah 3:11

The last line of this verse implies that material blessing can actually become a false sign of God's favor. Huge offerings are not necessarily a guarantee of the Lord's pleasure. We have a classic conflict of interest when those who are teaching prosperity are benefiting the most from the message.

I personally rejoice that the standard of living for pastors and ministers has risen in recent years, but the ministry must go the extra mile to present an image of financial integrity. God will bless those who give, even widows who give their last pennies to a spiritually and financially corrupt temple, but the keepers of the temple will be forever accountable.

Chapter Twenty-One

Common Ground

A CHRISTIAN LEADER who is not a participant in the charismatic renewal once asked me: "What do you feel is the difference between charismatics and non-charismatics? Your doctrinal position, as far as I can ascertain, seems to be nearly the same as ours. What do you think is at the heart of the controversy between us?"

Doctrinally, charismatics and non-charismatic evangelicals differ on only one major issue: the ministry of the Holy Spirit, specifically Spirit baptism. Even speaking in tongues, although it has been at center stage, is not the fundamental point of disagreement. Doctrinally, the differences are minimal. Charismatic theology is basically fundamental, evangelical, and orthodox. In an article on evangelicals in the Anglican Church, *Christianity Today* reported the findings of an eighteen-member study group organized to evaluate the growing charismatic movement in the Church of England. "The group concluded that non-charismatic evangelicals and

171

charismatics have more that unites them than divides them."[1]

If doctrine is not the key issue, if we share so many things in common, what is the problem? Because charismatics are noted for spiritual experiences that are different and non-traditional, suspicions and misunderstandings arise. Those who haven't shared in charismatic experiences react emotionally against them, and in response, charismatics become emotionally defensive when their cherished experiences with the Lord are criticized.

When I first began the research for this book I found myself reacting with emotion to what opponents of the charismatic renewal have written. I caught myself expressing wrong attitudes, but the Lord spoke definitely to my heart: "If you are not psychologically and theologically mature, if you cannot read objectively what others have written in opposition to your personal beliefs, then you are in no position to write a reply."

If we are intellectually honest, we must concede that everyone who holds firm convictions is stirred by the comments of those who disagree with him, but if we can keep reminding ourselves that many of the doctrinal disagreements among the brethren are relatively minor, and if we allow the Holy Spirit to keep our emotional responses in check, we will experience the unity of the Spirit, over whom we are disgracefully divided.

I have attempted to demonstrate from the Scriptures that charismatic teaching is tenable, and I have taken a biased stance on many issues. It has been my quest as a charismatic to know what I believe and why I believe it. Yet I realize that beneath the apologetic tangle there exists a far more important and fundamental principle—love. Speak the truth *in love*. Love builds up; knowledge puffs up. If I understand all mysteries and all knowledge, and have not love, I am nothing. Spiritual gifts are important, but love is supreme. •

I once heard a brother share that he believes the thirty minutes of silence in Revelation 8:1 is an expression of poetic justice. All the human clamoring, murmuring, and bickering is hushed by the overwhelming presence of the eternal God. Human history is a thicket of ignorance. We are quick to speak and slow to hear, but God is going to have the final word. *The* fruit of the Spirit is love—love for God, love for our brothers and sisters, and love for those who despise us. Love does not mean the compromise of personal conviction, but it does mean that we must be willing to lay down our lives for the brethren.

Much to my dismay, a close friend and brother in Christ left the charismatic renewal. He told me he was rethinking (rejecting, I believe) his former position. I have great difficulty understanding how someone who has become a partaker of the Holy Spirit could turn away, but there is a deeper lesson. In my heart I found myself asking, "Is my fellowship with my brothers and sisters based solely on doctrinal unity and the commonality of our spiritual experiences? Or is fellowship based on the unity of the Spirit and on our mutual relationship with Jesus Christ as our Lord and Savior?"

The love of God and the communion (the *koinonia*) of the Holy Spirit should be our initial point of reference as we fellowship with other believers. Christ must be preeminent in all things.

"And the Lord make you to increase and abound in love one toward another, and toward all men, even as we do toward you: To the end he may stablish your hearts unblamable in holiness before God, even our Father, at the coming of our Lord Jesus Christ with all his saints" (1 Thessalonians 3:12–13).

Love covers a multitude of sins—and doctrinal disagreements. Love is our common ground.

Footnotes

Chapter 1

1. Bob Campbell, *Baptism of the Holy Spirit: Command or Option?* (Monroeville, Pa.: Whitaker Books, 1973), p. 9.
2. Kenneth S. Kantzer, "Evangelicals and the Inerrancy Question," *Christianity Today*, 22 (April 21, 1978), p. 17.
3. Julia Duin, "What Does the Future Hold for Charismatic Renewal?" *Christianity Today*, 30 (May 16, 1986), p. 40.
4. C. I. Scofield, *The New Scofield Reference Bible* (New York, N.Y.: Oxford University Press, 1967), p. 930.
5. DeVern Fromke, *Unto Full Stature* (Indianapolis, Ind.: Ministry of Life Publishers, 1967), p. 215.
6. C. Peter Wagner, "A 'Third Wave' of the Power of God," *People of Destiny* (July/August 1985), p. 10.
7. Sharon E. Mumper, "Where in the World Is the Church Growing?", *Christianity Today* (July 11, 1986), p. 17.
8. Harold Lindsell, *Battle for the Bible* (Grand Rapids, Mich.: The Zondervan Corp., 1976).

Chapter 2

1. D. L Moody, *Secret Power* (Chicago, Ill.: Moody Press, n.d.), pp. 33–48.
2. F. B. Meyer, *Elijah: And the Secret of His Power* (Chicago, Ill.: Fleming H. Revell Co., n.d.), pp. 46–47.

Chapter 3

1. Don Basham, *A Handbook on Holy Spirit Baptism* (Monroeville, Pa.: Whitaker Books, 1969), p. 17.

2. D. L. Moody, *Secret Power* (Chicago, Ill.: Moody Press, n.d.), pp. 50–51.

3. Howard Snyder, *The Problem of Wine Skins* (Downers Grove, Ill.: InterVarsity Press, 1976), pp. 132–133.

4. Charles H. Usher, *Satan: A Defeated Foe* (Fort Washington, Pa: Christian Literature Crusade, n.d.), pp. 20–21.

5. Arthur Wallis, *Pray in the Spirit* (Fort Washington, Pa.: Christian Literature Crusade, 1972), p. 47.

Chapter 4

1. Don Basham, *A Handbook on Holy Spirit Baptism* (Monroeville, Pa.: Whitaker Books, 1969).

2. Bob Campbell, *Baptism in the Holy Spirit: Command or Option?* (Monroeville, Pa.: Whitaker Books, 1973), pp. 13–14.

3. Robert Glenn Gromacki, *The Modern Tongues Movement* (Philadelphia, Pa.: Presbyterian and Reformed Publishing Co., 1967), p. 106.

4. Anthony Hoekema, *What About Tongues-Speaking?* (Grand Rapids, Mich.: Baker Book House, 1973), p. 58.

5. For a thorough treatise on the weaknesses of Dispensationalism see *Prophecy and the Church* by Oswald T. Allis, published by Presbyterian and Reformed Publishing Co., 1974.

6. *The Amplified New Testament* (Grand Rapids, Mich.: Kregel Publications, 1958), p. 643.

7. George E. Gardiner, *The Corinthian Catastrophe* (Grand Rapids, Mich.: Kregel Publications, 1976), p. 28.

8. Howard Ervin, *These Are Not Drunken As Ye Suppose* (Plainfield, N. J.: Logos International, 1968), pp. 165–166.

9. Thomas A. Smail, *Reflected Glory* (Grand Rapids: Wm. B. Eerdman's, 1976), p. 42.

Chapter 5

1. Don Basham, *A Handbook on Holy Spirit Baptism* (Monroeville, Pa.: Whitaker Books, 1969).

2. Ralph Harris, *Spoken in the Spirit* (Springfield, Mo.: Gospel Publishing House, 1973).

3. Don Basham, *The Miracle of Tongues* (Old Tappan, N. J.: Fleming H. Revell, 1973).

4. Dennis Bennett, "The Gifts of the Holy Spirit," *The Charismatic*

Movement, ed. Michael T. Hamilton (Grand Rapids, Mich.: Wm. B. Eerdmans Publishing Co., 1975).

5. Robert Glenn Gromacki, *The Modern Tongues Movement,* (Philadelphia, Pa.: Presbyterian and Reformed Publishing Co., 1967), p. 67.

6. Marcus Bach, *The Inner Ecstasy,* (New York, N. Y.: The World Publishing Co., 1969), pp. 108–109.

7. William F. Arndt and F. Wilbur Gingrich, *A Greek-English Lexicon of the New Testament and Other Early Christian Literature* (Chicago, Ill.: University of Chicago Press, 1957), p. 395.

8. Johannes Behm, "Glossa," *Theological Dictionary of the New Testament,* I, ed. Gerhard Kittel, trans. Geoffrey W. Bromiley (Grand Rapids, Mich.: Wm. B. Eerdmans Publishing Co., 1972), p. 725.

9. Gromacki, p. 58.

10. Behm, p. 725.

Chapter 6

1. See Isaiah 28:10–12; 32:13; 44:3; Ezekiel 36:25–27; Joel 2:28–31; John 1:29, 33, 34; John 7:38; Luke 11:13; Acts 1:5–8.

2. Robert Glenn Gromacki, *The Modern Tongues Movement* (Philadelphia, Pa.: Presbyterian and Reformed Publishing Co., 1967), p. 89.

3. John Short, "I Corinthians," *Interpreter's Bible* (New York, N. Y.: Abingdon Press, 1953), Vol. 10, p. 197.

4. Don W. Hillis, *Tongues, Healing and You* (Grand Rapids, Mich.: Baker Book House, 1973), p. 24.

5. Horace S. Ward, "The Anti-Pentecostal Argument," *Aspects of Pentecostal Origins,* ed. Vinson Synan, (Plainfield, N. J.: Logos International, 1976), p. 116.

6. Ward, pp. 116–117.

7. Don Basham, *A Handbook on Holy Spirit Baptism* (Monroeville, Pa.: Whitaker Books, 1971), p. 64.

Chapter 8

1. Krister Stendahl, "The New Testament Evidence," Vinson Synan, ed., *Aspects of Pentecostal/Charismatic Origins* (Plainfield, N. J.: Logos, 1975), p. 53.

2. Kevin Ranaghan, *Catholic Pentecostals* (New York, N. Y.: Paulist Press, 1969), p. 199.

3. Howard Ervin, *These Are Not Drunken As Ye Suppose* (Plainfield, N. J.: Logos, 1968), p. 51.

Chapter 9

1. Dick Dugan, "We Dismantled Our Scarecrows," *Christian Life*, 39, (July 1977), pp. 26 ff.
2. Larry Christensen, *Speaking in Tongues, A Gift for the Body of Christ, Fountain Trust*, pp. 22–23, quoted in Don Basham, *A Handbook on Holy Spirit Baptism* (Monroeville, Pa.: Whitaker Books, 1969), p. 74.
3. Don Basham, *A Handbook on Holy Spirit Baptism* (Monroeville, Pa.: Whitaker Books, 1969), pp. 74–75.
4. Donald Burdick, *Tongues: To Speak or Not to Speak* (Chicago, Ill.: Moody Press, 1969), p. 84.
5. Stuart Bergsma, *Speaking With Tongues: Some Physiological and Psychological Implications of Modern Glossolalia* (Grand Rapids, Mich.: Baker Book House, 1965), p. 7.
6. Bergsma, p. 9.
7. John P. Kildahl, "Psychological Observations," Michael T. Hamilton, ed. *The Charismatic Movement* (Grand Rapids, Mich.: Wm. B. Eerdmans Publishing Co., 1975), pp. 124, 144.
8. James C. Logan, "Controversial Aspects of the Movement," in Hamilton, *The Charismatic Movement*, p. 39.
9. Howard Ervin, *These Are Not Drunken As Ye Suppose* (Plainfield, N. J.: Logos International, 1968), p. 124.

Chapter 10

1. A. T. Robertson, *Word Pictures in the New Testament*, Volume IX (Nashville, Tenn.: Broadman, 1930), pp. 96–97.
2. Don Basham, *Lead Us Not Into Temptation* (Old Tappan, N.J.: Chosen Books, 1986), p. 153.

Chapter 11

1. Thomas Smail, *Reflected Glory* (Grand Rapids, Mich.: Wm. B. Eerdmans, 1976), p. 13.
2. Dick Dugan, "We Dismantled Our Scarecrows," *Christian Life*, 39 (July 1977). p. 27.
3. James C. Logan, "Controversial Aspects of the Movement," *The Charismatic Movement*, Michael T. Hamilton, ed. (Grand Rapids: Wm. B. Eerdmans, 1975), p. 73.

4. Watson Mills, *Understanding Speaking in Tongues* (Grand Rapids, Mich.: Wm. B. Eerdmans, 1972), p. 76.

Chapter 12

1. Robert K. Johnston, "Of Tidy Doctrine and Truncated Experience," *Christianity Today*, 21 (February 18, 1977), pp. 10–14.

Chapter 13

1. George H. Williams and Edith Waldvogel, "A History of Speaking in Tongues" in *The Charismatic Movement*, ed. Michael T. Hamilton, (Grand Rapids, Mich.: Wm. B. Eerdmans Publishing Co., 1975), pp. 61, 63, 64.

2. Jules Lebreton and Jacques Zeiller, *The History of the Primitive Church*, Vol. I (New York, N. Y.: Macmillan Co., 1949), p. 557.

3. Justin Martyr, *Second Apology*, 6.

4. B. J. Kidd, *A History of the Church to A.D. 461*, Vol. I (Oxford: Clarendon Press, 1922), p. 290.

5. Kenneth Scott Latourette, *A History of Christianity*, Vol. I (New York, N. Y.: Harper and Row, 1975), p. 128.

6. Philip Carrington, *The Early Church*, Vol. II (Cambridge: The University Press, 1957) p. 267.

7. Irenaeus, *Against Heresies*, 11, 32.4.

8. *Ante-Nicene Fathers*, I, p. 409.

9. Irenaeus, *Against Heresies*, III, 11.9.

10. Irenaeus, *Against Heresies*, II, 31.2.

11. Irenaeus, *Against Heresies*, II, 6.1.

12. Tertullian, *To Scapula*, IV.

13. Tertullian, *A Treatise on the Soul*, XLVII.

14. Tertullian, *To Scapula*, IV.

15. Tertullian, *Against Marcion*, v. 8.

16. Tertullian, *Against Marcion*, v. 8.

17. Carrington, p. 168.

18. Carrington, p. 143.

19. Eusebius, *History*, v. xiii

20. Kidd, p. 290.

21. Tertullian, *Against Praxeas*, I₁.

22. Origen, *Against Celsus*, I. 46.

23. Origen, *Against Celsus*, I. 46.

24. Origen, *Against Celsus*, I. 67.

25. Cyprian, *Epistle LXXV*, 16.

26. Benedicta Ward, trans., *The Sayings of the Desert Fathers* (London: A. R. Mowbray, 1975) p. 43.

27. Ward, p. 104.

28. Ward, p. 130.

29. Ward, p. 140, 141.

30. Ward, p. 126.

31. Eusebius, *History*, v. 7.1.

32. Brian Baily, Karl Coke, and Charles Welty, "Church Fathers Speak: Historical Reaction to Spiritual Gifts," *Acts* (Jan.–Feb. 1977) p. 11.

33. Baily, Coke, and Welty, p. 12.

34. Henry H. Ness, *The Baptism with the Holy Spirit: What Is It?* (Springfield, Mo.: Bill Britton, n.d), p. 14.

35. Ness, pp. 14–15.

36. For this portion of this historical survey, I am indebted to Edward Barry of Phoenix, Arizona, a graduate of Asbury Theological Seminary, a participant in the charismatic renewal and an avid student of Church history.

37. John Thomas Nichol, *The Pentecostals* (Plainfield, N. J.: Logos International, 1971).

38. Stanley H. Frodsham, *With Signs Following* (Springfield, Mo.: Gospel Publishing House, 1946).

Chapter 14

1. Gordon Clark, *First Corinthians: A Contemporary Commentary* (Nutley, N. J.: Presbyterian and Reformed Publishing Co., 1975), p. 254.

Chapter 15

1. Albert Barnes, *Notes, Explanatory and Practical, on the Epistle to the Romans* (New York, N. Y.: Harper and Brothers, Publishers, 1872), pp. 293–294.

2. W. E. Vine, *An Expository Dictionary of New Testament Words* (Old Tappan, N. J.: Fleming H. Revell Co., 1966), p. 221.

3. Kenneth Taylor, *The Living Bible* (Wheaton, Ill.: Tyndale House Pub., 1973), p. 925.

4. William F. Beck, "The New Testament in the Language of Today," in *The Four Translation New Testament* (Minneapolis, Minn.: World Wide Publications, 1966), p. 487.

5. Albert Barnes, *Notes, Explanatory and Practical, on the First Epistle to the Corinthians* (New York, N. Y.: Harper and Brothers, Publishers, 1848), pp. 278–279.

6. Gerhard Friedrich, ed., *Theological Dictionary of the New Testament*, trans. Geoffrey W. Bromiley (Grand Rapids, Mich.: Wm. B. Eerdmans Publishing Co., 1972), Vol. VI, p. 791.

7. Friedrich, p. 795.

8. Friedrich, p. 815.

9. Richard C. Trench, *Synonyms of the New Testament* (Grand Rapids, Mich.: Wm. B. Eerdmans Pub. Co., 1880), p. 23.

10. Gerhard Kittel, ed., *Theological Dictionary of the New Testament*, trans. Geoffrey W. Bromiley (Grand Rapids, Mich.: Wm. B. Eerdmans Pub. Co., 1972), Vol. III, pp. 686–688, 692–693.

11. Kittel, p. 696.

12. Kittel, pp. 703, 710–711.

13. Michael Harper, *Prophecy: A Gift for the Body of Christ* (London: The Fountain Trust, 1966), p. 8.

Chapter 16

1. Krister Stendahl, "The New Testament Evidence," in *The Charismatic Movement*, ed. Michael T. Hamilton (Grand Rapids, Mich.: Wm. B. Eerdmans Pub. Co., 1975), p. 56.

2. Joseph Henry Thayer, *Greek-English Lexicon of the New Testament* (Grand Rapids, Mich.: Zondervan Corp., 1973), p. 574.

3. A. T. Robertson, *Word Pictures in the New Testament*, 6 vols., (Nashville, Tenn.: Broadman Press, 1931), 4:505.

4. Albert Barnes, *Notes, Explanatory and Practical, on the Epistles of Paul to the Ephesians, Philippians, and Colossians* (New York, N. Y.: Harper and Brothers, Publishers, 1859), p. 119.

5. G. I. Williamson, unpublished articles.

6. Steven Barabas, "Zion," *Zondervan Pictorial Bible Dictionary* (Grand Rapids, Mich.: Zondervan Corp., 1969), p. 914.

7. Matthew Henry, *Commentary on the Whole Bible*, 3 vols. (Marshallton, Del.: Sovereign Grace Publishers, n.d.), 3:1024.

Chapter 17

1. McCrossan, T. J., *Bodily Healing and the Atonement* (Youngstown, Oh.: Clement Humbard, 1930).

2. Rotherham, *The Emphasized Bible.*

3. McCrossan, p. 19.

4. McCrossan, p. 29.

5. McCrossan, p. 33, 34.

6. McCrossan, p. 34.

7. McCrossan, p. 50.

8. Sturz, Harry A., *The Byzantine Text-Type and New Testament Textual Criticism,* (Nashville, Tenn.: Thomas Nelson Publishers, 1984).

Chapter 19

1. Steve Scott and Brooks Alexander, "Inner Healing," *Spiritual Counterfeits Journal,* Vol. 4, No. 1, April 1980, pg. 12.

2. Sanford, R. Loren, "A Note About Visualization," *Elijah House Newsletter,* Nov. 1985.

Chapter 21

1. "Nottingham '77: Evangelicals Eye Unity" (anon.), *Christianity Today,* Vol. 21 (May 20, 1977), p. 45.

Selected Bibliography

Arndt, William F. and Wilbur F. Gingrich. *A Greek-English Lexicon of the New Testament and Other Early Christian Literature.* Chicago: University of Chicago Press, 1957.

Bach, Marcus. *The Inner Ecstasy.* New York: The World Publishing Co., 1969.

Bailey, Brian; Karl Coke; and Charles Welty. "Church Fathers Speak: Historical Reaction to Spiritual Gifts," *Acts* 1(Jan.–Feb. 1977): 7–16.

Basham, Don. *A Handbook on Holy Spirit Baptism.* Monroeville, Pa.: Whitaker Books, 1969.

———. *Lead Us Not Into Temptation.* Old Tappan, N.J.: Chosen Books, 1986.

———. *Ministering the Baptism in the Holy Spirit.* Monroeville, Pa.: Whitaker Books, 1971.

———. *The Miracle of Tongues.* Old Tappan, N.J.: Fleming H. Revell, 1973.

Barnes, Albert. *Notes, Explanatory and Practical, On the First Epistle to the Corinthians.* New York: Harper and Brothers, Publishers, 1848.

———. *Notes, Explanatory and Practical, On the Epistles to the Ephesians, Philippians, and Colossians.* New York: Harper and Brothers, Publishers, 1859.

———. *Notes, Explanatory and Practical, On the Epistle to the Romans.* New York: Harper and Brothers, Publishers, 1872.

Beck, William F. "The New Testament in the Language of Today," in *The Four Translation New Testament.* Minneapolis: World Wide Publications, 1966.

Bennett, Dennis and Rita. *The Holy Spirit and You.* Plainfield, N.J.: Logos International, 1971.

Bergsma, Stuart. *Speaking with Tongues: Some Physiological and Psychological Implications of Modern Glossolalia.* Grand Rapids: Baker Book House, 1965.

Brewster, P. S. *The Spreading Flame of Pentecost.* London: Elim Publishing House, 1970.

Bruce, F. F. *Commentary on the Book of Acts.* Grand Rapids: William B. Eerdmans Publishing Co., 1954.

Brunner, Frederick Dale. *A Theology of the Holy Spirit.* Grand Rapids: William B. Eerdmans Publishing Co., 1974.

Buntain, D. N. *Holy Ghost and Fire.* Springfield, Mo.: Gospel Publishing House, 1956.

Burdick, Donald. *Tongues: To Speak or Not to Speak.* Chicago: Moody Press, 1969.

Campbell, Bob. *Baptism in the Holy Spirit: Command or Option?* Monroeville, Pa.: Whitaker Books, 1973.

Carrington, Philip. *The Early Church,* Vol. II. Cambridge: The University Press, 1957.

Clark, Gordon. *First Corinthians.* Nutley, N.J.: Presbyterian and Reformed Publishing Co., 1975.

Cockburn, Ian. *Baptism in the Holy Spirit: Its Biblical Foundation.* Plainfield, N.J.: Logos International, 1971.

Criswell, W. A. *The Baptism, Filling and Gifts of the Holy Spirit.* Grand Rapids, Mich.: Zondervan Corp., 1973.

Dalton, Robert Chandler. *Tongues Like As of Fire.* Springfield, Mo.: Gospel Publishing House, 1945.

Dugan, Dick. "We Dismantled Our Scarecrows," *Christian Life* 39 (July 1977): p. 26ff.

Dyer, Luther B., ed. *Tongues.* Jefferson City, Mo.: Le Roi Publishers, 1971.

Ervin, Howard M. *These Are Not Drunken As Ye Suppose.* Plainfield, N.J.: Logos International, 1968.

——. *. . . And Forbid Not To Speak With Other Tongues.* Plainfield, N.J.: Logos International, 1971.

Frodsham, Stanley H. *With Signs Following.* Springfield, Mo.: Gospel Publishing House, 1946.

Fromke, DeVern. *Unto Full Stature.* Indianapolis: Ministry of Life Publishers, 1967.

Gardiner, George E. *The Corinthian Catastrophe.* Grand Rapids: Kregel Publications, 1976.

Gee, Donald. *All with One Accord.* Springfield, Mo.: Gospel Publishing House, 1961.

————. *Concerning Spiritual Gifts.* Springfield, Mo.: Gospel Publishing House, n.d.

Gillies, George and Harriet. *A Scriptural Outline of the Baptism in the Holy Spirit.* Monroeville, Pa.: Banner Publications, n.d.

Gromacki, Robert Glen. *The Modern Tongues Movement.* Philadelphia: Presbyterian and Reformed Publishing Co., 1967.

Hamilton, Michael T., ed. *The Charismatic Movement.* Grand Rapids: William B. Eerdmans Publ. Co., 1975.

Harper, Michael. *Prophecy: A Gift for the Body of Christ.* London: The Fountain Trust, 1966.

Harris, Ralph. *Spoken in the Spirit.* Springfield: Gospel Publishing House, 1973.

Henry, Matthew. *Commentary on the Whole Bible,* 3 vols. Marshallton, Del.: Sovereign Grace Publishers, n.d.

Hillis, Don W. *Tongues, Healing and You.* Grand Rapids: Baker Book House, 1973.

Hoekema, Anthony A. *What About Tongues-Speaking?* Grand Rapids: William B. Eerdmans Pub. Co., 1966.

Iverson, Dick. *Holy Spirit Today.* Portland: Center Press, 1976.

Jeter, Hugh. *By His Stripes.* Springfield, Mo.: Gospel Publishing House, 1977.

Johnston, Robert K. "Of Tidy Doctrine and Truncated Experience," *Christianity Today* 21(February 18, 1977): pp. 10–14.

Kantzer, Kenneth S. "Evangelicals and the Inerrancy Question," *Christianity Today* 22 (April 21, 1978): p. 17ff.

Kelsey, Morton T. *Healing and Christianity.* New York: Harper and Row, 1973.

Kidd, B. J. *A History of the Church to A.D. 461,* Vol. I. Oxford: Clarendon Press, 1922.

Kildahl, John P. *The Psychology of Tongues.* New York: Harper and Row, 1972.

Kittel, Gerhard and Gerhard Friedrich, eds. *Theological Dictionary of the New Testament,* 10 vols. Translated by Geoffrey W. Bromily. Grand Rapids: William B. Eerdmans Publishing Co., 1972.

Koch, Kurt. *The Strife of Tongues.* Berghausen, Germany: Evangelization Publisher, n.d.

Latourette, Kenneth Scott. *A History of Christianity,* Vol. I. New York: Harper and Row, 1975.

Lebreton, Jules, and Zeiller, Jacques. *The History of the Primitive Church*, Vol. I. New York: Macmillan Co., 1949.

Lindsell, Harold. *Battle for the Bible*. Grand Rapids, Mich.: Zondervan Corp., 1976.

Lindsey, Gordon. *Thirty Objections to Speaking in Other Tongues*. Dallas: Christ for the Nations, 1972.

Lockman Foundation. *The Amplified New Testament*. Grand Rapids: Zondervan Publishing House, 1958.

McArthur, John. *The Charismatics*. Grand Rapids: The Zondervan Corp., 1978.

McGee, J. Vernon. *Talking in Tongues*. Los Angeles: The Church of the Open Door, n.d.

Meyer, F. B. *Elijah: And the Secret of His Power*. Chicago: Fleming H. Revell Co., n.d.

Mills, Watson. *Understanding Speaking in Tongues*. Grand Rapids: William B. Eerdmans Pub. Co., 1972.

Moody, D. L. *Secret Power*. Chicago: Moody Press, n.d.

Ness, Henry H. *The Baptism of the Holy Spirit: What Is It?* Springfield, Mo.: Bill Britton, n.d.

Nichol, John Thomas. *The Pentecostals*. Plainfield, N.J.: Logos International, 1971.

Nickel, Thomas. *In Those Days*. Monterey Park, Cal.: Great Commission International, 1962.

"Nottingham '77": Evangelicals Eye Unity," *Christianity Today* 21(20 May 1977): pp. 44–45.

Prince, Derek. *Baptism in the Holy Spirit*. Fort Lauderdale, Fla.: Study House Publications, n.d.

———. *Purposes of Pentecost*. Fort Lauderdale, Fla.: Study Hour Publications, n.d.

Ranaghan, Kevin and Dorothy. *Catholic Pentecostals*. New York: Paulist Press Deus Books, 1969.

Rea, John, ed. *Layman's Commentary on the Holy Spirit*. Plainfield, N.J.: Logos International, 1972.

Roberts, Alexander, and Donaldson, James, eds. *The Ante-Nicene Fathers*, 10 volumes. Grand Rapids: William B. Eerdmans, 1985.

Robertson, A. T. *Word Pictures in the New Testament*, 6 vols. Nashville: The Broadman Press, 1930.

Rose, Wil. "What's Right For You?" *Christian Life* 39(July 1977): p. 24.

Ryrie, Charles. *Balancing the Christian Life.* Chicago: Moody Press, 1969.

Sanford, R. Loren, "A Note About Visualization," *Elijah House Newsletter*, Nov. 1985.

Schaff, Philip, and Wace, Henry. *Nicene and Post-Nicene Fathers of the Christian Church, Second Series, 14 volumes. Grand Rapids: William B. Eerdmans, 1982.*

Schaff, Philip. *The Nicene and Post-Nicene Fathers*, 14 volumes. Grand Rapids: William B. Eerdmans, 1983.

Scofield, C. I., ed. *The New Scofield Reference Bible.* New York: Oxford University Press, 1967.

Scott, Steve and Alexander, Brooks, "Inner Healing," *Spiritual Counterfeits Journal*, Vol. 4, No. 1, April 1980.

Sennet, James F., "A Questionable Faith," *The Wittenburg Door*, No. 83, June/July, 1985.

Sherrill, John. *They Speak with Other Tongues.* New York: McGraw-Hill Book Co., 1964.

Short, John. "I Corinthians," in *The Interpreter's Bible*, Vol. 10. New York, N.Y.: Abingdon Press, 1953.

Smail, Thomas. *Reflected Glory.* Grand Rapids: William B. Eerdmans Pub. Co., 1976.

Snyder, Howard A. *The Problem of Wine Skins.* Downers Grove, Ill.: InterVarsity Press, 1976.

Stagg, Frank, Glenn E. Hinson, and Wayne E. Oates. *Glossolalia.* New York: Abingdon Press, 1967.

Synan, Vinson, ed. *Aspects of Pentecostal/Charismatic Origins.* Plainfield, N.J.: Logos International, 1975.

Taylor, Kenneth. *The Living Bible.* Wheaton: Tyndale House Publishers, 1971.

Tenney, Merrill C., ed. *Zondervan Pictorial Bible Dictionary.* Grand Rapids, Mich.: Zondervan Publishing House, 1969.

Thayer, Joseph Henry. *Greek-English Lexicon to the New Testament.* Grand Rapids: Zondervan Publishing House, 1973.

Theissen, Henry C. *Lectures in Systematic Theology.* Grand Rapids: William B. Eerdmans Publishing Co., 1974.

Trench, Richard C. *Synonyms of the New Testament.* Grand Rapids: William B. Eerdmans Publishing Co., 1880.

Truscott, Graham. *Power of His Presence*. Burbank, Cal.: World Map Press, 1972.

Usher, Charles H. *Satan: A Defeated Foe*. Fort Washington, Pa.: Christian Literature Crusade, n.d.

Vine, W. E. *An Expository Dictionary of New Testament Words*. Old Tappan, N.J.: Fleming H. Revell Co., 1966.

Wallis, Arthur. *Pray in the Spirit*. Fort Washington, Pa.: Christian Literature Crusade, 1972.

Ward, Benedicta, trans. *The Sayings of the Desert Fathers*. London: A. R. Mowbray, 1975.

Williams, J. Rodman. *The Era of the Spirit*. Plainfield, N.J.: Logos International, 1971.